BUILDING AND RESTORING CIVIC CAPACITY:

THE OBAMA ADMINISTRATION'S
FEDERAL-LOCAL PARTNERSHIP WITH DETROIT
(2011-2016)

December 3, 2016

The Executive Office of the President

Table of Contents

Table of Contents 2

Executive Summary 3

I.   The Evolution of the Detroit Federal Working Group: From Crisis Response to Building Capacity 8

II.   Neighborhood Stabilization 11

III.   Resilience & Sustainability 17

IV.   Workforce Development & Training 21

V.   Transportation 25

VI.   Economic Development 29

VII.   International Affairs 33

VIII.   Policing & Public Safety 37

IX.   Observations from Detroit: Key Lessons and the Path Forward 41

X.   Recent Federal Commitments to Detroit 43

Acknowledgements 59

Executive Summary

"There is still plenty of work, but can you feel the difference. You can feel something special happening in Detroit."
—President Barack Obama, January, 2016 [1]

"The idea that we're not going to do everything in our power to bring back, not just a great city, but an iconic city was unthinkable. Detroit is like its people -- it's resilient."
—Vice President Joe Biden, September, 2015

Despite Detroit's legacy as an icon of American industry and innovation, the Motor City found itself grappling with substantial and long-simmering problems when President Obama took office. Its famous auto industry was in crisis and had largely left the city proper, its population had declined for half a century, vital city services were not being delivered, and the City government was hurtling towards bankruptcy. People worried about Detroit's future.

President Obama committed the federal government to the region's recovery within weeks of taking office, demonstrating his confidence in the American worker—and the City of Detroit—by providing temporary federal assistance to rescue the auto industry. This assistance paid off: The industry avoided catastrophic failure, returned to profitability, and added over 646,000 US jobs.

Still, the President recognized that Detroit's mounting crisis extended well beyond the troubles of the auto industry. In 2011, the President intensified the federal commitment to Detroit by assigning a team of top federal talent to partner with the Mayor, state agencies, business, philanthropy and community stakeholders. The federal effort focused on: (1) understanding the complexities of Detroit's crisis; (2) directly engaging citizens and stakeholders; and (3) delivering tailored assistance and identifying resources that could help Detroit get back on its feet. This effort has continued through 2016, and its structure has adapted to meet changing needs.

The Detroit Engagement

The progress described in this report belongs to the people of Detroit. From the outset, local leaders set the priorities for the federal engagement, and without Detroiters' resilience and sustained commitment, none of the progress made would have been possible. The federal team worked shoulder-to-shoulder with local leaders, including Mayors Bing and Duggan, the city's private and philanthropic sectors, and state and community leaders.

To the Detroit partnership, the federal government brought its convening power, technical expertise and other resources. The federal team worked to co-create solutions and look for ways to help Detroit accomplish its objectives faster, more effectively and more efficiently than it would have otherwise. In a few cases, the City entrusted the federal team with a central role in convening the relevant problem-solvers to address a high priority initiative. Detroit competed for federal awards, not always successfully. But the determination of the city to keep improving is captured in a favorite local slogan: "Detroit Hustles Harder."

The contributions featured in this report fall into seven issue areas, reflecting the City's priorities:

---

[1] http://www.fox2detroit.com/news/local-news/77918659-story

Issue Area	Examples of Progress Made by Federal-Local Partnership: 2011-2016
NEIGHBORHOOD STABILIZATION • **Blight spreading in the city's neighborhoods**: During the recession and bankruptcy, Detroit home values crashed and abandonment spread block-by-block. The community-led Blight Task Force identified 85,000 blighted/vacant properties posing environmental and public safety risks. • **Scarce access to loans for home purchases and renovations.** Low appraised values hindered banks from making loans sufficient to cover the cost of rehabilitation, which held back the recovery of property values. • **Loans to develop apartments not available.**	• **Over 10,000 blighted homes demolished using green methods, with 50-100 taken down every week.** Michigan allocated Detroit over $260 million from the Treasury Department's Hardest Hit Fund for demolition and greening; HUD provided $13 million. EPA's technical advice minimized environmental risks. • **Zero Percent Home Rehab program launched by City and nonprofits, with $6.6 million in existing funds from HUD and $4 million in private sector funding.** Over 300 renovation loans have closed. • **New Detroit Home Mortgage covers the "appraisal gap."** DFWG convened banks, foundations and the state to develop a new loan product of up to $75,000 that covers costs above low appraised values. 163 credit-screened homebuyers are searching for homes. • **HUD financed early multifamily projects in midtown, and from 2014-2016, financed construction or rehabilitation of 1400+ units citywide.**
RESILIENCE & SUSTAINABILITY • **City government had limited capacity to consider sustainability projects.** Staff focused on crisis response and restoring core public sector functions. • **Over half of 88,000 streetlights were dark.** • **Flooding overwhelmed Detroit's aging storm water infrastructure:** In August 2014, historic flooding caused $1 billion in property damage to 118,000 home owners and businesses. • **City parks needed investment:** Many urban parks were neglected due to financial pressures and poor maintenance.	• **City will launch a Sustainability Office in 2017.** Office will identify and implement sustainable solutions (e.g. energy audit of city buildings). • **Highly efficiency LED lights installed citywide:** DOE provided technical assistance resulting in the City selecting a new lighting system that saves 46 million kW of energy and $3 million annually. • **Green infrastructure upgrades will address flood risks:** The City and the federal team identified sustainable, cost-effective ways to reduce flooding risks. HUD provided $8.9 million for smart recovery, including green infrastructure investments; EPA advised on how vacant lots could increase water absorption. • **New 10-acre solar facility to be opened in a decommissioned Park:** DOE provided technical assistance on the viability of urban projects. • **$5 million of scheduled EPA riverfront parks investments accelerated by 5 years:** Federal agencies synchronized their investments to match the City's new park improvement master plan.
WORKFORCE DEVELOPMENT & TRAINING • **Detroit has the highest unemployment rate of the 50 largest US cities.** • **Weak connection between workforce initiatives and employers.** • **Difficulty Reintegrating Returning Citizens into Workforce:** 3,000 Detroiters return	• **New Workforce Development Board of 30+ employers and stakeholders aligns programming with job market demands.** DOL provided "best practices" consulting and information on federal workforce initiatives. • **DOL awarded $5 million for job training, including correctional facilities.** • **Detroit won $2 million in competitive grants to support the expansion of the City's summer jobs program by 42 percent, to 8,000 students.**

Issue Area	Examples of Progress Made by Federal-Local Partnership: 2011-2016
from incarceration every year, often with poor employment prospects.	• **State, federal and local agencies are collaborating to align workforce training and social services for SNAP (food assistance) participants.** • **Michigan and the City of Detroit have teamed with USDA optimize utilization of federal workforce development resources.**
TRANSPORTATION & MOBILITY	
• Buses frequently delayed, with an aging and broken fleet. • Inadequate regional transit coordination: Most Detroiters work in the city, while most city jobs are held by suburbanites. Public transit does not extend beyond city boundaries. Detroit metro is the largest in US without a regional transit system. • Legacy of car-oriented urban development: Detroit's development was not designed for pedestrians, bicyclists and public transit.	• **Bus ridership up 1 million in the last year, with improved reliability and more routes:** DOT provided $25 million grant for 80 new, greener buses. • **In 2017, a new streetcar system will link downtown to emerging neighborhoods.** DOT awarded $37.2 million and provided extensive technical assistance to support the streetcar system; the project used more than $41 million in New Market Tax Credits from US Treasury. • **Encouraged launch of new Regional Transit Authority to link transit systems:** DOT provided technical assistance and $6.4 million grant. • **Detroit adopts pedestrian/bike-friendly "smart growth" approach and launches Mobility Office:** DOT awarded $10 million for non-motorized upgrades such as new bike lanes. DOE helped plan for a Mobility Office, and DOE will assign staff from Argonne National Laboratory.
ECONOMIC DEVELOPMENT	
• Limited civic capacity for crafting economic development strategy: Responding to the city's emergency needs limited its capacity to develop forward-looking strategies. Detroit's manufacturing sector needed infrastructure investments and strategic planning to compete in the global marketplace. • Detroit's economic crisis hit small businesses and underserved communities hardest.	• **Funding for manufacturing strategy:** In 2012, EDA funded an industrial corridor study, and in 2016 EDA followed with $3.2 million for infrastructure and $800k for a business attraction team. As a result, the city landed a $95 million investment from an automotive supplier. • **Two new manufacturing hubs located in Detroit**: In 2014, Detroit won a DOD lightweight-materials lab, bringing $140 million of research investment. In 2015, DOE co-located a composites research facility. • **HUD worked with the City to make $2.9 million available for the "Motor City Match" quarterly competition for businesses and building owners.** • **Supporting minority entrepreneurs:** MBDA awarded $2.8 million to fund a business development center and advanced manufacturing resources. • *Advance Michigan* **coalition forms and creates a regional manufacturing strategy that earns Detroit preference in federal competitions.**
INTERNATIONAL AFFAIRS	
• Despite the presence of global industries, a port, an iconic cultural legacy, and a large foreign-born population in the region, Detroit lacked a global engagement strategy and structure. • Untapped potential to connect Detroit to international opportunities.	• **City's first global engagement strategy:** DFWG is developing the first strategy and structure for global engagement to boost economic activity in Detroit. The State Department detailed a full-time senior staff to Detroit for this effort. • **Raised Detroit's international profile:** DFWG structured the Mayor's first international mission to Japan with Detroit companies; staffed his second mission to China; and organized missions to Cuba and Europe.

Issue Area	Examples of Progress Made by Federal-Local Partnership: 2011-2016
• **Detroit's global reputation suffered during its municipal bankruptcy.** The city's misfortunes overshadowed its recovery. • **Refugee resettlement efforts were unstructured and neglected.**	Highlighted Detroit at the President's 2016 Global Entrepreneurship Summit and the Venice Biennale, and helped nominate Detroit for the "UNESCO City of Design" designation. • **New strategy to help resettle 300 refugees in Detroit:** DFWG worked with the Mayor, stakeholders, and federal agencies on a refugee resettlement strategy. City launched an Office of Immigrant Affairs.
POLICING & PUBLIC SAFETY • **In 2003, Detroit Police Department entered into a consent decree with DOJ to reform unlawful policing and detention practices.** • **Detroit lacked the resources and expertise to address violent crime and build trust between police and community.**	• **Police Department identified its priorities and needs, for example body-worn cameras, and DOJ supplied funding, training and peer exchanges that have begun to reduce crime.** DPD focused on youth violence; obtaining technology assessments; hiring and retaining police officers; training crime analysts; and developing effective grant strategies. • **To build public trust, policing data now routinely published online.**

Detroit and the "Community Solutions" Approach

The Detroit engagement exemplifies the federal government's **"Community Solutions"** approach that provides a "one-stop shop"/customer service orientation that changes how the federal government works with and responds to the needs of local communities. It calls for an integrated federal government to align resources, cultivate working relationships, and streamline communications. The approach aims to meet communities' immediate needs and better position local leaders to address long-term objectives.

This Community Solutions approach is now employed by variety of federal-local partnerships serving over 1,800 places across the country. From Fresno to Baltimore, federal leaders are working across traditional agency lines and offering hands-on, locally relevant assistance.

The Evolving Federal-Local Partnership in Detroit

The Detroit federal-local partnership evolved as the City leaders shifted from crisis response to rebuilding internal capacity. What began as a federal inter-agency effort progressed to an uncommonly high engagement with senior White House leaders, reflecting the severity of Detroit's situation.

> **Agency-Led Support for a Distressed City (2011-2013):** In 2011, federal agencies deployed staff to the City of Detroit through the "Strong Cities, Strong Communities" ("SC2") initiative. The City directed the embedded federal SC2 team to provide intensive, hands-on assistance fulfilling core municipal functions.
>
> **Detroit Federal Working Group: Crisis Response (2013-2014):** As Detroit's finances deteriorated, leading to municipal bankruptcy in 2013, the White House escalated its assistance to a Presidential priority with direct, cabinet-level engagement. The expanded federal team continued to provide technical assistance; identified new, unspent, or repurposed federal funds; and developed strategies that targeted the City's self-identified needs.
>
> **Detroit Federal Working Group: Capacity Building (2015-2016):** In 2015, the federal team turned to the Mayor's longer-term priorities. As the City attracted talented leaders to its

municipal agencies, the federal team offered education and technical assistance so that they could work most effectively on the Mayor's goals.

Effective Federal Strategies in Detroit

The federal team's successful efforts involved a core set of strategies:

- **Provide technical assistance (in various forms)**: Advice may take the form of subject-matter experts who can review strengths, flag promising developments, and identify gaps, unmet needs, and areas for improvement; share best practices from other cities; offer technology expertise; or help navigate federal processes.

- **Establish peer-to-peer networks with similarly situated local governments**: These peer relationships are valuable – whether for one conference call or project, or for ongoing, regular discussions. The federal government's view across municipalities makes it an effective convener and match-maker for those conversations.

- **Scout for federal opportunities and adapt federal programs to local needs**: Federal agencies offer myriad programs, some on an annual cycle and others as one-time pilot programs. The federal team may be able to find relevant programs suited to local priorities.

- **Convene senior business and nonprofit stakeholders, along with state and local government, to solve problems**: As an independent party, the federal team brings a neutral perspective and its outside knowledge to problem solving. The DFWG often worked with multiple state and local agencies and brought business and community stakeholders into deliberations. At times, the federal team convened stakeholders that would not have otherwise met.

- **Organize visits and meetings between federal and local officials to highlight local needs**: Attention from high-level agency officials brings visibility and urgency to local issues.

- **Anticipate future opportunities**: Federal teams may be aware of emerging issues that are not yet a priority but offer long-term value, e.g. sustainability, mobility, international affairs.

- **Draw on "best practices" to assist the City's strategic planning**: In support of the Mayor's priorities, the DFWG provided technical assistance to strategic planning.

- **Sustain attention and focus**: The federal team focused on Detroit's recovery for several years, rather than treating it as an episodic engagement. Sustained, on-the-ground staff attention made its support more responsive to city needs and fast-changing economic conditions. City officials felt greater confidence turning to a trusted and informed partner.

About This Report

This report focuses on *what* the federal partnership contributed to the city's recovery and *how* the federal-local partnership helped build local capacity to achieve its long-term objectives. The "Recent Federal Contributions" section lists federal contributions to Detroit's revitalization that resulted from the federal-local partnership. This report cannot list all of the federal assistance to Detroit, which includes annual funding that is set by national funding formulas, such as for Medicaid, Medicare, public education, etc., nor the recurring grant opportunities and staff support that was not directly related to the federal-Detroit initiative.

I. The Evolution of the Detroit Federal Working Group: From Crisis Response to Building Capacity

"Every time we've brought a City priority to the federal government—from revitalizing neighborhoods to improving bus service—we've found a willing and helpful partner."

—Detroit Mayor Mike Duggan, December, 2016

While the President's commitment to Detroit's recovery began with the rescue of the American auto industry, he also recognized that helping Detroit overcome the substantial challenges it faced would take a focused, place-based collaboration with the City government and local stakeholders.[2]

The Administration's direct engagement with the City of Detroit can be organized into three phases:

I. Agency-Led Support for a Distressed City (2011-2013)

The federal engagement first ramped up in 2011, when Detroit and six other cities were chosen though a competitive process to participate in the Administration's new *Strong Cities, Strong Communities* initiative (SC2). The SC2 initiative was supported by the Department of Housing and Urban Development and included multiple agencies collaborating to assist distressed communities.

Strong Cities, Strong Communities provides a new model of federal-local partnership "to strengthen neighborhoods, towns, cities and regions around the country by strengthening the capacity of local governments to develop and execute their economic visions and strategies."[3] Department of Justice attorney Portia Roberson led Detroit's SC2 team who were embedded in the City Hall. The SC2 team networked across agencies and levels of government, as well as with stakeholders outside government.

The SC2 team's efforts were supplemented by the work of the SC2 Fellows. The Fellowship Program provided SC2 cities with highly motivated, early or mid-career professionals who work for two years in mayor's offices or local government agencies.[4] Fellows worked on strategic projects proposed by the City.

II. Detroit Federal Working Group: Crisis Response (2013-2014)

After decades of mounting fiscal challenges, Detroit filed for bankruptcy on July 18, 2013. Recognizing the gravity of Detroit's situation, the President asked National Economic Council Director Gene Sperling to lead an all-government effort to assist Detroit's recovery.

---

[2] The President demonstrated his commitment to place-based solutions in the first year of his Administration, when he directed the Office of Management and Budget, the Domestic Policy Council, the National Economic Council, and the Office of Urban Affairs to conduct a comprehensive review of federal programs impacting places, the first review of its kind in thirty years.

[3] Barnes, Melody, "Announcing Strong Cities, Strong Communities," July 11, 2011.

[4] The SC2 Fellowship program was developed by the Department of Housing and Urban Development, managed and implemented by the German Marshall Fund Partnership, and funded by a gift from the Rockefeller Foundation, matched by local commitments.

Director Sperling invited a wide range of expertise to craft a rapid federal response. In July, he convened the agency representatives on the "SC2 Council" to hear what challenges and opportunities those agencies identified in Detroit. Director Sperling and his team also reached out to civic leaders and outside experts with Detroit-specific expertise. Throughout this process, the State of Michigan served as a critical partner, providing expertise and coordinating planned state and federal recovery efforts.

In September 2013, Director Sperling led a delegation to Detroit with the Secretary of Housing and Urban Development, the Attorney General, and the Secretary of Transportation, where they organized a citywide meeting with local business, philanthropic, community, faith and government leaders. At the meeting, they announced up to $300 million in new, repurposed or freed-up federal funds for the City. This White House leadership raised the visibility and the importance of the recovery effort.

The President appointed Don Graves, Jr., the Executive Director of the President's Council on Jobs and Competitiveness, to serve as the Administration's point-person for Detroit and empowered him to tap federal agencies at the cabinet-level for support. Graves and agency representatives from Treasury, HUD, the Department of Transportation, and the Department of Energy partnered with Detroit's City Hall and community stakeholders, maintaining an active, on-the-ground presence. The team identified opportunities for Detroit to apply for federal funding and unlocked existing federal funding that had not been spent due to reduced municipal capacity.

The team provided high-quality technical assistance and used the Administration's convening power. Local leaders prized the technical assistance customized to their needs: Detroit's then-Chief Operating Officer told federal officials, "Your technical assistance is worth even more than your money."

For example, in November 2013, the White House Office of Science and Technology Policy convened a "Tech Team" of leading civic technologists in Detroit to recommend specific ways the City could use technology to advance its recovery efforts and improve city services. The Mayor embraced the recommendations and recruited one of the leading technologists to serve as Detroit's Chief Information Officer and focus on implementing them.

Not every intervention was high-profile. The Administration's team also facilitated informal introductions and coordinated partnerships linking locally-led initiatives like the Blight Removal Task Force[5] to relevant federal experts; Detroit's economic development team with the nation's leading financial institutions; and elected City leaders with senior Administration officials. The team routinely attended community meetings, church gatherings, events at local schools and businesses to explain the federal government's work and to understand community needs.

III.   The Detroit Federal Working Group: Capacity Building (2015-2016)

In January 2015, President Obama appointed Cliff Kellogg, from the Executive Office of the President, to lead the Detroit Federal Working Group (DFWG). The President tasked the group with continuing the high-level federal engagement in Detroit, emphasizing capacity-building that will enable the city to continue its recovery beyond the end of his Administration.

---

[5] Detroit's Blight Removal Task Force was a privately-funded effort, announced alongside federal efforts in September 2013, to determine the scope of the city's blight problem and identify solutions for it.

The DFWG is currently an initiative of the White House's Community Solutions Team created to advance the federal government's commitment to partnering effectively with communities.

The DFWG includes five deputy directors from federal agencies:

- The Department of Commerce—Economic Development Administration
- The Department of Energy (detailed to the Office of the Vice President)
- The Environmental Protection Agency
- The Department of Labor
- The Department of State (detailed to the White House National Economic Council)

Each deputy is an experienced federal employee with a portfolio of issues in his or her area of expertise. Deputies consult weekly with their City counterparts and visit Detroit at least once every couple of weeks. The State Department deputy re-located to Detroit full-time as continuous, on-the-ground support. These deputies received additional support from the White House Community Solutions Team, the Office of the Vice President, and the Department of Transportation. The DFWG meets monthly with representatives from more than 20 federal agencies to discuss the progress of federal initiatives. The monthly meeting features a Detroit speaker on local initiatives.

II.   Neighborhood Stabilization

"Downtown may be the heart of Detroit, but the neighborhoods are its soul."
—Maurice Cox, Director of Planning for the City of Detroit

When the Administration began its direct assistance to Detroit, the city had been hemorrhaging residents for decades. Property values declined rapidly in the wake of the housing and credit crisis. By 2013, Detroit's community-led Blight Task Force identified 85,000 blighted or vacant properties in the city—representing 22 percent of all parcels. The blight and abandonment problems were particularly glaring in its neighborhoods, where abandoned and dilapidated houses threatened even the strongest communities. The federal-Detroit collaboration sought to counter this contagion by: (1) providing resources to the State for the safe and effective elimination of existing blight; (2) innovating with private-sector partners to address the market gaps failures that discouraged home renovation and home-buying in Detroit; and (3) coordinating federal resources to help the city strategically shore up "tipping point" neighborhoods.

Today, Detroit's population has stabilized; preliminary data suggest a small net population increase last year. Detroit attracts national attention for using environmentally-friendly methods to demolish more than 10,000 blighted structures. New opportunities exist for financing home-buying and renovation. The City's neighborhood investments are coordinated with the expertise and resources of numerous federal agencies, ranging from the Department of Agriculture to the National Endowment for the Arts. While more work is required to strengthen Detroit's neighborhoods, Detroit is now able to expand its attention beyond the provision of basic public services to longer-term, strategic redevelopment.

Federal Team Strategies

- Freed up federal resources to fund the demolition and greening of vacant and abandoned houses in order to stop the spread of blight and prevent further housing foreclosures.

- Convened discussions among federal, state, and local officials to share expertise on public health risks and best practices in demolition.

- Sustained engagement with the City for over 21 months as the City, the Detroit Building Authority and their contractors worked out new demolition protocols.

- Worked with banks, foundations and the state to design a new mortgage pool to solve the "appraisal gap" that hindered access to home finance.

- Assessed and approved HUD multifamily housing finance programs in early projects along the Woodward corridor.

- Recognized the opportunity to build a network of federal-local working relationships based on the City's neighborhood redevelopment process.

- Organized a "funding charrette"—a meeting of stakeholders—to introduce federal agencies to Detroit's neighborhood revitalization strategy and to forge working relationships among federal-local partners.

Detroit's Completed Demolitions

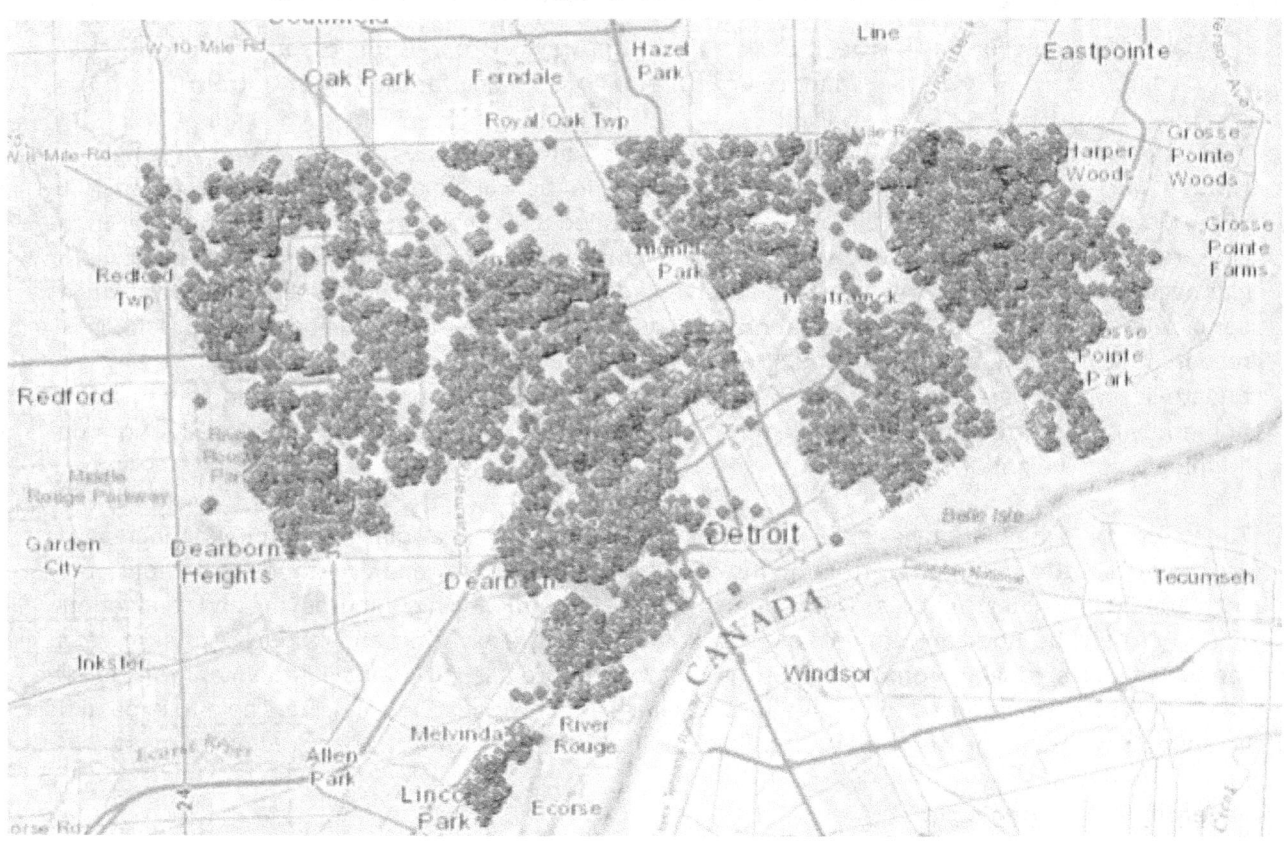

Blight Demolition to Prevent Foreclosures

Detroit's blight problem accelerated when home values collapsed during the housing crisis of 2006-2009. Many homeowners abandoned their homes, leading to mortgage and tax foreclosures, followed by scavenging of the property, as well as arson and crime. Abandonment spread block-by-block as residents lost confidence in the city's future. Despite pockets of progress in select neighborhoods, most homes are worth significantly less than their 2006 peak.

In 2013, the federal team worked with local leaders to launch the Detroit Blight Task Force. Led by business and community leaders, this task force focused on developing a practical strategy to eliminate blight. Many observers considered this task daunting due to the longstanding and complex nature of Detroit's blight problem. Backed with substantial philanthropic commitments and access to federal expertise, the Blight Task Force[6] gathered data for effective, evidence-based problem-solving. The Task Force produced a public report on the scale and scope of the blight, noting each abandoned home.

---

[6] The Steering Committee for the Blight Task Force included representatives from the Center for Community Progress; City of Detroit; Office of the Emergency Manager, City of Detroit; Data Driven Detroit; Detroit Land Bank Authority; DTE Energy; Loveland Technologies; Michigan Nonprofit Association; Michigan State Housing Development Authority; New Hope Community Development; Rock Ventures Family of Companies; The Kresge Foundation; The Skillman Foundation; US Department of Housing & Urban Development; US Department of Treasury.

This mapping exercise revealed the scale of the challenge—the report identified 85,000 blighted or vacant properties out of 380,000 parcels citywide, many posing considerable environmental risks. The report presented the problem clearly for problem-solvers who communicated Detroit's need.

The Detroit federal team identified the potential application of an existing program—Treasury's Hardest Hit Fund (HHF)—to stop the spread of blight and stabilize home values. The federal team provided evidence that this strategy would prevent avoidable home foreclosures, the primary goal of the HHF program. After reviewing the evidence and Michigan's proposal for a new statewide blight elimination program, the Treasury Department approved the use of HHF for demolition.

In 2016, Detroit's Congressional delegation, led by Michigan Senator Stabenow, successfully advocated for additional HHF funding in Congress to keep the progress going. To date, the Michigan State Housing Development Authority has allocated more than a $260 million from its HHF allocation to Detroit for the removal of blighted homes. Over 10,000 blighted homes have been demolished, with 50 to 100 more coming down each week. Property values are starting to rise as the blight recedes. A recent economic study demonstrated that every $1 spent on demolitions in Detroit raised adjacent property values by $4, a remarkable return on the government's investment. [7]

Other states facing similar blight/depopulation challenges also adopted this use of HHF to prevent a domino effect of home abandonment.

Demolition Methods: Creating a Model to Protect Public Health

The City was in bankruptcy receivership when it reassessed what demolition practices would be used to remove over 100 homes per week. Knowing the City faced intense pressure to pursue environmental shortcuts, the federal team explained the public health and environmental hazards of various demolition methods. The federal team explained how other cities had approached blight demolition, noting instances where struggling cities had failed to consider the long-term costs of "cheap" blight demolition practices that ultimately created expensive environmental liabilities and hindered reinvestment.

When the City decided to explore environmentally responsible demolition practices, the DFWG and EPA convened 80 stakeholders for a green demolition workshop. The City organized a working group that quickly updated existing demolition contracts to require safer, cleaner methods. The City overhauled the entire system of demolitions *before* it became a public health issue.

---

[7] http://www.crainsdetroit.com/article/20151006/NEWS/151009893/report-use-of-u-s-blight-elimination-funds-increased-detroit-home

Improved demolition practices mean that:

- Fewer children with asthma will be exposed to fugitive dust and fewer workers exposed to asbestos fibers;

- Certified clean soil is brought in to fill demolition sites, which are then greened with low maintenance grass seed or clover;

- During rainstorms, the newly-vacant lots soak up water like a sponge rather than overwhelming the sewer system and flooding basements.

Demolition of Vacant Public Housing that Symbolized Detroit's Blight Problem

In 2012, the Detroit Housing Commission received a $6.5 million dollar emergency grant from HUD to demolish the Frederick Douglass Homes (also known as the Brewster-Douglass Housing projects), a vacant public housing development spanning over 18 acres that had long been a symbol of blight and a haven for serious crime. Demolition began in September 2013 and HUD continues to provide expertise and support.

Zero Percent Home Loan Program: Helping Homeowners Repair their Homes

The majority of Detroit's homes were constructed before 1950, and many homes require modernization. Before Mayor Duggan's administration, the City addressed this need by disbursing HUD Community Development Block Grant (CDBG) dollars as outright grants to homeowners. In 2014, the Mayor asked for a different strategy. The Mayor wanted to end the windfall "lottery ticket" method of giving away CDBG money, and instead, create a loan fund that recycles repaid loans so that more people could benefit.

In response, the City of Detroit and LISC devised the Zero Percent Interest Home Loan Program with financial assistance from HUD. The program provides interest-free loans to Detroiters up to $25,000 (repayable over 10 years) so homeowners can repair their homes. The loans are commonly used for electrical repairs, furnace replacement, roof replacement, plumbing, door and window replacement, restoration or maintenance of porches and structural support. HUD worked with the City to obtain several program waivers to use CDBG funds along with Bank of America funds to subsidize the interest on the loans. The Zero Percent loan program started with $8 million in loan funds and $3.6 million in administrative funds from a mix of CDBG and private capital.

The program is especially important to support property values in tipping point neighborhoods. One of the waivers assures that loans are available to everyone in an affected area: Low-income homeowners can apply no matter where they live; residents with higher incomes can apply if they live in designated revitalization areas of the City. If a resident does not qualify based on credit, the program will help them improve their credit score with free credit counseling. Since its launch in March 2015, the program has accepted 1,586 applications, of which 516 were pre-approved and 164 have already completed repairs. The average loan size is $16,800.

Detroit Home Mortgage: Solving the "Appraisal Gap"

A significant obstacle to accessing home mortgages in Detroit is the "appraisal gap." The appraisal gap exists because banks determine how much to lend homeowners based, in part, on the sales prices of similar homes. When home values are extremely low—and in Detroit, the average price of a home is approximately $40,000—the loan amount is not enough to cover the cost of a refurbished home. In Detroit, bank lending data shows that almost 40 percent of declined loans were primarily due to low appraised values. Homeowners must cover this "appraisal gap" with their own cash out-of-pocket, however most homeowners are not prepared to tackle a fixer-upper with their own funds. Developers in the business of buying and fixing up homes also shy away from the City because they are concerned that buyers will not find a loan. The end result is that the appraisal gap brings mortgage lending almost to a standstill. In 2014, 88 percent of home sales were for cash, which limits the pool of available buyers and the amount they can pay for a home.

At the Mayor's request, the DFWG convened banks, foundations and the state of Michigan to look for solutions. In June 2015, the group committed to overcoming the appraisal gap.

CEOs from five local banks pledged their support and formed a mortgage working group. The federal team maintained the focus and the momentum of the group with weekly meetings to monitor progress. A banking consultant with capital markets experience joined the group. The group designed the Detroit Home Mortgage (DHM) to raise property values by pairing a bank's first mortgage with a second mortgage held by a nonprofit CDFI. Homebuyers can borrow up to $75,000 above a home's appraised value, provided they met FHA credit standards and complete mandatory homebuyer education. Each of the five participating banks committed to originate mortgages using the same underwriting guidelines. Seven banks have committed to investing in the pool of second mortgages.

The working group raised philanthropic social investment capital from The Kresge Foundation to cover losses in the event a homebuyer suffered an adverse economic crisis beyond her control. The state of Michigan invested funds to buy down the interest rate. The DFWG identified regulatory experts to review the final program design.

> *"This is a game-changer for Detroit. We are confident that Detroit Home Mortgage will increase homeownership in the city of Detroit… With an opportunity to get a home mortgage, qualifying homeowners and homebuyers have a real opportunity to buy and renovate a house in the city and make it a home."*
>
> —Detroit Mayor Mike Duggan

In February 2016, the five bank CEOs announced the DHM product with extensive press coverage. Through October, over 1,200 DHM inquiries have come to the banks, over 150 applications are credit-screened, allowing the homeowner to shop for a home to buy. The first 11 DHM mortgages have closed.

New FHA Multifamily Developments Coming On-line

As property values declined during the recession, new development of apartment buildings nearly came to a standstill. By the early 2010s, HUD's Detroit field office believed in the city's economic recovery. Beginning with smaller projects in the Mid-town area, HUD established a track record of facilitating the financing for multifamily developments, restoring confidence in the market.

Progress on attracting and retaining Detroit residents is apparent: in five years from 2009 to 2014, HUD's Federal Housing Administration (FHA) guaranteed financing for 165 units of new multifamily housing in the City. In the next two years, FHA played an instrumental role in financing over 900 *new* multifamily housing units. The new housing developments include a mixture of market-rate and affordable units. HUD also provided FHA-mortgage insurance for the rehabilitation of 622 existing affordable housing units.

15

While more work must be done to spur housing development outside of downtown and Mid-town, Detroit's real estate market has improved significantly. Whereas FHA-backed loans were the primary source of financing in 2011 for multi-family developments, today, private sector activity is stronger than it has been in several decades.

Priority Planning Neighborhoods: Fitzgerald Neighborhood

When property values fell in Detroit in 2006, housing developers found the cost to fix up a house often exceeded its sales price. Renovating homes one-by-one inevitably leaves many other homes in poor conditions on the same or adjoining blocks. The same weak investment pattern affects small businesses making facility investments. The challenge is to focus investment into concentrated areas for redevelopment.

In August 2016, Mayor Mike Duggan announced a new neighborhood-based revitalization strategy in seven target areas. In the first neighborhood, Fitzgerald, the City designated a one-quarter square mile area as a "Priority Planning Neighborhood" (PPN). PPN locations are selected based, in part, on the availability of publicly-owned houses and land to sell as a bundle. In each PPN, the City will select a developer to implement a holistic redevelopment plan that includes the rehabilitation of existing vacant housing and a landscaping plan for green spaces. The Fitzgerald RFP offered approximately 200 vacant houses to developers to renovate for-rent or for-sale.

The City's PPN plan creates an organized process that enables federal agencies to apply their tools and expertise. In September 2016, the DFWG organized a "funding charrette" attended by federal, state and foundation officials. The charrette is a group meeting of stakeholders to address a common problem. The City's Planning Department presented its vision of creating "20 minute" neighborhoods in the city. These neighborhoods will be denser, walkable, bike-able communities where residents can satisfy all essential needs within a 20-minute walk or bike ride: schools, parks, public transit and basic retail shopping. The federal attendees, in turn, explained how their agencies' programs could apply to the Fitzgerald neighborhood. The discussion spanned a wide range of elements, from housing, to small business development, to options for mobility, to transforming vacant land into green space. Planned follow-up in 2017 will ensure that new connections can be maintained and strengthened. A recent grant award of $4 million from a national philanthropic partnership called "Reimagining the Civic Commons" will give the effort a major lift.

The City's plan created a "landing place" for federal resources. It established a predictable process within a strategic vision. This allowed agencies to see their programs in a larger framework. The City will announce the selection of the Fitzgerald master development team in December 2016. Three more neighborhood design processes commenced in October. While the outcomes of this process remain to be seen, early-stage engagement looks promising, and philanthropic resources are expected to become available as well, due to the quality of the planning and partnerships.

III.   Resilience & Sustainability

Environmental leadership can be difficult to pursue during an economic crisis. By thinking practically and in terms of how the city manages its resources over the long-term, the federal team has helped Detroit chart a path to a vastly more sustainable future.

At the outset of the federal engagement, the challenges facing Detroit were practical and immediate: half of its street lights were out; flooding overwhelmed the aging storm-water infrastructure; and public parks were neglected. The City needed to prioritize fulfilling core municipal functions over undertaking a conscious effort to improve environmental quality.

Cognizant of this pressure, the federal team pursued solutions to the problems that could liberate the city from ongoing cycles of stopgap measures. This approach has been tangibly validated by improvements in street lighting, energy infrastructure, public parks, and storm-water management. Seeing the value of considering sustainability across many City agencies, the Mayor has endorsed the launch of Detroit's Office of Sustainability in 2017.

Federal Team Strategies

- Provided technical assistance to explain how light-emitting diode (LED) light installation saves costs and helped the City craft the technical specification for the new technology.

- Discussed with the electric utility the viability of an urban solar facility and identified the technical assistance needed to make Detroit a successful site choice.

- Accelerated the timeline of federal investments in three riverfront parks to synchronize with Detroit's master plan.

- Identified best practices in green infrastructure projects as a cost-effective response to storm-water infrastructure (e.g. sewer) vulnerabilities revealed during flood.

- Provided assistance to the City's efforts to develop objectives, a staffing strategy, and work plan for a new Office of Sustainability.

City Builds Long-term Institutional Capacity for Sustainability Management

By focusing on green solutions that provide practical benefits, the City came to appreciate the cost savings from sustainability initiatives. The City's new Sustainability Office will coordinate resources across its agencies. For example, the new Sustainability Office will analyze the City's automotive needs and move towards a more efficient fleet of hybrid and electric vehicles. The Office will assess energy savings from consolidating various City office buildings, taking into account energy efficiency.

Detroit's new partnership with Argonne National Laboratories will provide resources for sustainable problem-solving. The DFWG introduced Argonne representatives to Detroit officials and facilitated the signing of an MOU framework in 2016. Under the MOU, the national laboratory will support the City with ongoing technical advice and embedded staff to address sustainability concerns ranging from energy storage to transportation.

Outdated Street Lights Replaced with Energy-Efficient Lighting

When the President took office, less than half of Detroit's 88,000 street lights were operating due to staff shortages, theft, and deteriorating infrastructure. In 2013, the Detroit Public Lighting Authority (PLA) was incorporated and made plans to replace Detroit's streetlight system with conventional high-pressure sodium lights. In 2014, the Mayor made new PLA board appointments and tasked it modernizing the faltering street lighting infrastructure. Simultaneously, the Department of Energy team analyzed the City's needs and presented the Mayor and PLA with a data-driven case for a new type of lighting, energy-efficient light-emitting diodes (LEDs). Detroit's Mayor recognized that the energy and maintenance savings would offset the higher cost of LED lighting installation, and he directed the PLA to make the switch. As PLA crafted its request for proposals to contractors interested in overhauling the lighting infrastructure, the Department of Energy team assisted so that Detroit received high-quality lighting. DOE experts remained a resource for questions throughout the proposal evaluation process.

As a result of the collaboration between the Department of Energy and the City, Detroit's streets are lit by LED lights, almost a year ahead of schedule. When the final 65,000th LED streetlight is installed, it is estimated that the City will save $2.94 million annually in electricity costs, and 45.6 million kilowatt-hours in energy. An estimated 41 tons of nitrogen oxide will be reduced, along with 40,418 tons of carbon dioxide, and 1.5 pounds of mercury.

This DOE technical assistance to Detroit served as a model for a new federal program, the High Performance Outdoor Lighting Accelerator, announced by the President.

New Solar Energy Facility Transforms a Decommissioned Park

In 2015, a pioneering solar energy field was not an obvious answer to two problems facing Detroit: the difficulty of attracting energy infrastructure investment and what do with a struggling neighborhood's unmaintained, decommissioned park.

During the Energy Secretary's May 2014 visit to Detroit, the Mayor inquired about locating an urban solar project in Detroit. The DFWG learned that the region's major electric utility planned to request proposals for a utility-scale solar project, likely to be in a rural setting.

The utility executives expressed doubts about the viability of a smaller Detroit location, but said that the project's prospects could be improved by assigning a City Hall point-person. The City promptly assigned a staffer who worked with the utility to identify potential locations that met its size and technical requirements.

The DFWG identified the National Renewable Energy Laboratory as a source for technical assistance. Federal experts reviewed the utility's RFP specifications to ensure that the utility was aware of best practices. The federal experts partnered with a local non-profit to develop site selection criteria. The City committed $250K of HUD-provided Community Development Block Grant funds to the project's construction.

The federal team's attention to City priorities, coupled with a willingness to think creatively, yielded remarkable dividends. In September 2016, the Energy Secretary, Mayor Duggan, utility executives and neighborhood residents gathered to break ground on the 10-acre site at O'Shea Park, a decommissioned park in a blighted neighborhood. DOE estimates the solar facility will produce 3,500 MWh's each year, valued at approximately $125k per year.

The Mayor and the utility agree that it will be the first of many such solar opportunities.

Accelerated Improvements for Riverfront Parks

When Mayor Duggan took office, Detroit's parks had been neglected for years, a casualty of strained City budgets. The Mayor moved quickly to institute a masterplan for park improvements, with municipal investments occurring in 2017. Unaware of the Mayor's plan, the federal agencies continued with their own plan to pay for riverfront park improvements beginning in 2022 at the earliest.

Reviewing the masterplan during a routine visit, the federal team saw the potential to synchronize federal and municipal park investments. The EPA team member pointed out that accelerating the start of federal investments by five years would increase the return on the federal investment. Today, the City, the US Environmental Protection Agency and the National Park Service are coordinating investments to restore parks and will construct new wildlife habitat in the three upper riverfront parks (AB Ford, Lakefront East, and Mariner Park). This outcome was possible thanks to the City's master plan for parks and the federal partners' thoughtful work to realign their resources so that three separate initiatives could be rolled out simultaneously.

Floods Alert Detroit to Need for Resilient Storm-water Management Infrastructure

In August 2014, historic flooding devastated Detroit, causing millions of gallons of untreated sewage to overflow the sewers into the Great Lakes and resulting in at least $1.1 billion in property damage to 118,000 homeowners and businesses. The natural disaster's impact laid bare a harsh reality: the city's aging storm-water infrastructure, dating back more than a century in some cases, posed a serious, ongoing economic and public health liability.

The City faced a resource management problem, namely, how to address the problems posed by aging infrastructure cost-effectively. The DFWG presented options for green infrastructure investments in terms that reflected the city's concerns: Rebuilding the old system was financially untenable. Green improvements would reduce flooding risk, qualify for federal funding and provide ancillary benefits such as open space, urban agriculture plots, and habitat preservation. Today, Detroit has embraced green infrastructure investments to manage storm water and meet the mandates of the Clean Water Act.

In August 2015, the City of Detroit was awarded $8.9 million from the HUD Community Development Block Grant Program funding (via the Declared Disaster Recovery Fund) to further increase neighborhood resiliency through demolitions using environmentally sound methods and greening vacant lots. Multiple projects in Detroit are considering potential green infrastructure solutions. Projects ranging from planned roads, parks, parking lots, roofs, and buildings are all being evaluated for green infrastructure opportunities. With additional support from non-profit organizations, vacant lots are increasingly being used as sponges to soak up water that would otherwise run into the Great Lakes and flood basements during rain storms.

IV.   Workforce Development & Training

Detroit faces stark workforce challenges. Of the fifty largest cities in the United States, Detroit has the lowest percentage of employed residents: about half of Detroiters between the ages of 16 and 64 are unemployed, compared to the national average of 25 percent.[8] Only 258,000 jobs exist within the city limits, significantly less than its working population. Almost three-quarters of the jobs that do exist in Detroit are held by residents from outside the city.

Prior to 2015, the City's workforce development and training activities were administered by Detroit Employment Solutions Corporation (DESC), a nonprofit that handled the *public* workforce system's services to Detroit adults, dislocated workers and youth. DESC capably managed state and federal grant programs, but many believed that the workforce training programs had neglected to develop meaningful connections to employers and to the more than 400 private workforce training organizations operating in the city. As a result, the Mayor believed that restructuring could improve the placement of trainees in jobs.

Detroit seized an opportunity with the reauthorization of the Workforce Innovation and Opportunity Act (WIOA) to overhaul its workforce development board. The federal team, able to scan for best practices and navigate the suite of available federal resources, helped the City take greater advantage of federal initiatives addressing Detroit priorities such as improving services at job centers, the re-integration of citizens returning from incarceration, and increasing the number of summer jobs for young Detroiters.

Federal Team Strategies

- The Secretary of the Department of Labor (DOL) met with Mayor Duggan and the Governor to discuss local conditions and the DOL's relevant programs.

- DFWG facilitated a visit to Baltimore's Johns Hopkins Hospital and to a Montgomery County, Maryland correctional facility to learn about "best practices" for employment programs for returning citizens.

- The DOL Secretary visited Detroit to encourage participation by businesses and federal agencies in the City's summer jobs program.

- The federal team provided technical assistance for scaling up Detroit's summer jobs program and identified the opportunity to get partial reimbursement for private funds expended in conjunction with the City's workforce development program.

- The DFWG helped Detroit locate expertise on programs for out-of-school youth and on how to organize one-stop enrollment in job training programs

New Workforce Board Connects Job Training to the Private-Sector

In October 2015, Mayor Duggan introduced the new Mayor's Workforce Development Board (WDB), aligned directly with implementing the WIOA. WIOA requires cities like Detroit to have an integrated

---

[8] http://www.freep.com/story/news/local/michigan/detroit/2016/01/16/detroit-aims-cut-unemployment/78858112/

strategy for workforce development and social services, as well as an emphasis on serving out-of-school youth.

Mayor Duggan appointed 36 members to the WDB. The WDB includes Chief Executive Officers from many of Detroit's largest companies, organized labor unions and nonprofit training organizations. The Department of Labor-Employment and Training Administration Deputy Assistant Secretary attended a board meeting to offer training on board development and strategic planning.

The WDB engages employers to set the training standards for entry-level positions. The WDB will develop a system to monitor those matriculating through a workforce system of more than 400 private training organizations in Detroit.

DOL also provided funding to integrate the adult services provided through the American Job Centers and to comply with new WIOA requirements. DOL committed technical assistance funds to the City to support its efforts to streamline registration for multiple job-training programs as well as create a youth services model that includes in-school youth.

"Best Practices" Discussions Lead to Funding for Returning Citizens

The commitment of federal expertise, up to the Secretarial level, has provided Detroit with exposure to best practices for tackling its most pressing civic issues.

During an early 2015 visit to Detroit, the Secretary of Labor described several communities that offered career training services in correctional facilities with encouraging results. These services are geared toward inmates' successful re-entry by focusing on soft skill development, resume-writing classes, interview training and job-search skills. The prospect of improved reentry outcomes appealed to Detroit leaders, who were aware that Detroit reintegrates over 3,000 formerly-incarcerated citizens each year. Within a few weeks, workforce development leaders from the State of Michigan, City of Detroit and a local staffing agency visited the correctional facility in Montgomery County, Maryland and the Johns Hopkins Hospital in Baltimore that has had success hiring returning citizens for certain positions.

Inspired by this model, the State of Michigan applied for and received a $5 million demonstration grant to support a project serving youth and young adults. The grant pays for two American Job Centers, one at the Detroit Reentry Center and another at the Macomb County Correctional Facility. Almost 900 Detroiters will receive education, training and career services including case management and connections to companies the construction, technology, manufacturing, transportation and logistics sectors. Participants will also have the opportunity to participate in pre-apprenticeship training that can lead to a registered apprenticeship.

My Brother's Keeper Summit to Connect Underserved Youth to Employment Pathways

> "*This program is one of the best I've seen. You* have *the current President of the United States behind it, you have the business community behind it,* [*and*] *you have the philanthropic community behind it.*"
> —Quicken Loans founder and Chairman Dan Gilbert[9]

In launching the My Brother's Keeper initiative in 2014, President Obama called on communities and leaders in the private sector to develop their own strategies to help young people reach their full potential. In November 2016, responding to this call to action, the non-profit My Brother's Keeper Alliance, the City of Detroit / MBK-Detroit, the Kellogg Foundation, the Campaign for Black Male Achievement, and the Detroit Regional Chamber co-hosted the "Invest in Youth: Pathways to Success Career Summit." The day-long event provided over 1,400 youth, including young men of color, the opportunity to interview with more than 40 employers, participate in career preparation and leadership development training, connect to community agencies, get criminal record expungement services, as well as haircuts, ties and blazers. More than 300 participating young Detroiters received jobs on the spot.

Capacity Building to Support Summer Jobs

Summer jobs can introduce young people to the norms and expectations of holding a job. During the summer of 2015, Detroit employed 5,600 youth in Grow Detroit's Young Talent Initiative (GDYT). GDYT-enrolled youth work for six weeks, on average 20 hours a week, and they receive 12 hours of work-readiness training and as well as 24 hours of training on financial literacy. In 2016, the City pledged to increase the program to 8,000 youth, a 43 percent increase. DOL, with support from the White House Summer Ambassador Initiative, provided technical assistance for the expanded summer job program. HUD offered technical assistance on how to use Community Development Block Grants to fund summer employment programs. The City used $1 million of CBDG funds for summer jobs programs in 2015.

To further the Administration's commitment to summer job opportunities, DOL launched the Summer Jobs and Beyond grant program. DESC successfully competed for a $2 million award. This funding will continue to expand the summer jobs program by providing paid work experiences for 1,000 youth through June 2018.

Aligning Workforce and Nutritional Assistance Programs

The U.S. Department of Agriculture's (USDA) Supplemental Nutrition Assistance Program Employment and Training (SNAP E&T) program helps participants gain the skills, training, and work experience necessary to increase their employment prospects. For the *Detroit SNAP E&T Initiative*, staff from USDA teamed with DOL, Detroit's Workforce Development Board, and the State of Michigan so that 200 SNAP recipients receive the greatest possible access to the range of existing federal, state and local programs.

The SNAP E&T program offers intensive case management; access to short-term training opportunities that provide credentials; subsidized employment; on-the-job training, and apprenticeships. Support services are also provided, such as transportation assistance, childcare, and books, trade tools, and uniforms. USDA supported this Detroit initiative with technical assistance and $1 million in additional

---

[9] http://www.prnewswire.com/news-releases/my-brothers-keeper-alliances-pathways-to-success-opportunity-summit-connects-young-detroiters-with-career-opportunities-300365998.html

funds (unused SNAP funds were reallocated to the State of Michigan which provided them to this initiative). In addition, USDA provided a waiver allowing federal funds to be used for wage subsidies. In promoting this initiative, federal and local staff made a concerted effort to dispel the mistaken notion that enrolling in job training would affect benefit eligibility.

Helping Detroit Access USDA Workforce Development Resources for SNAP Participants

Through USDA's SNAP E&T program, states can be reimbursed for 50 percent of certain qualifying workforce development expenses paid by an eligible, third-party provider. This program is commonly known as accessing "50/50 funds". The Mayor asked DFWG how Detroit and the State of Michigan could maximize its use of 50/50 funds to supplement Detroit's workforce budget. To support state efforts, USDA created the *SNAP to Skills* program to provide states with the knowledge, tools and resources necessary to build more effective and employment-driven SNAP E&T programs. One element of *SNAP to Skills* is a module on utilization of the 50/50 funds reimbursement. USDA invited Michigan to participate in *SNAP to Skills*.

As a result of this collaboration, Michigan applied for and was approved to add two third-party providers in Detroit (Southwest Solutions and Focus: Hope) whose commitments will be matched with $500,000 in 50/50 funds from USDA's Food and Nutrition Service.

V.   Transportation

Detroit faced considerable public transportation challenges when the federal team began its work in 2011. The majority of Detroit residents work outside the city, and yet 25 percent of Detroit households do not own a vehicle. Despite this apparent need for reliable mass transit, Detroit bus passengers endured frequent schedule delays due to an aging, poorly maintained fleet of vehicles.[10] Most bus routes do not extend beyond city or town boundaries, and many suburban communities exercise their legal right to 'opt-out' of a regional transit system.

The federal team supported local efforts to create new transportation options such as streetcars, the Inner Circle Greenway for bikes and pedestrians and to improve existing ones. Over the last 12 months, the annual bus ridership in Detroit has increased over 1 million trips, an 11 percent increase. With its new hybrid buses, the Detroit Department of Transportation has updated the old route map and begun 24-hour service on major thoroughfares. The new Regional Transit Authority has published its master plan to extend Bus Rapid Transit into the suburbs. While significant challenges remain, Detroit's transportation system is becoming more reliable, better integrated into a regional plan and more sustainable.

Federal Team Strategies

- Encouraged Detroit leaders to develop a means for regional transportation planning and followed up with funding and technical assistance for the Regional Transit Authority.

- Provided Detroit with technical assistance regarding federal funding for municipal bus purchases. Helped Detroit maximize impact of its transportation budget and get buses sooner by identifying opportunities to tap into the unused portion of other municipalities' pending bus orders.

- Provided extensive technical assistance in conjunction with Detroit's push to improve bus operations.

- Provided extensive technical assistance to advance planning and construction of the M-1 streetcar system

- Publicized Detroit's commitments to accessible public transportation and walkable neighborhoods and pedestrian-friendly transportation infrastructure by inviting Detroit's planning director to present to senior DOT leadership.

- Encouraged Detroit agencies to consider federal competitions where the application process requires the collaboration across institutional silos. This planning process generated awareness of opportunities in the emerging field of mobility and "smart" infrastructure.

---

[10] The city of Detroit covers a larger land area than Boston, San Francisco and Manhattan combined.

Bus Service Improvements

"When I started here, there were days where 40 percent of the buses just didn't show up. We didn't have enough drivers; we couldn't repair the buses; the buses were so old they weren't salvageable..."

—Detroit Mayor Mike Duggan

By 2014, Detroit's bus system was in poor shape. On an average day, just 70 percent of the buses scheduled to be on the road would be functional. The average age of the bus fleet was 12 years, and the buses had not been well-maintained. Preventative maintenance simply did not occur almost one-third of the time. The buses that did pull out of the garage in the morning frequently ran late.

When Mayor Duggan was elected, new management at the Detroit Department of Transportation (DDOT) invited the federal government to ramp up its technical assistance. The new DDOT management took greater advantage of U.S. Department of Transportation's (DOT) expertise, which helped give rise to a collaborative coaching dynamic that characterizes many of the DOT's most successful community partnerships. For example, at one point DDOT experienced major performance issues with the large doors to their new bus maintenance facility after just five years of use. The federal team worked with DDOT to remedy the door problem, and showed flexibility on federal useful-life rules that normally would have prevented using new funding for at least 16 years.

In 2015, Detroit submitted a successful bid for a $25 million dollar DOT grant for new bus purchases. To help Detroit stretch the benefit of the grant award, the federal team searched extensively for opportunities to save on new buses and, eventually, helped Detroit acquire 80 new buses. New bus purchases typically come with a lead time of a few years. The federal team aided Detroit in finding other municipalities with pending bus orders that included a few unused orders where Detroit could piggyback. Detroit received its buses by mid-2016 and immediately put them in service.

With new management and new buses, Detroit's bus system is showing signs of improvement. Ridership is up 11 percent from 2014. The bus fleet recently met its goal of operating all buses that were scheduled to be in service that day. On-time service is up, while accidents are down.

Supporting Detroit's New M-1 Street Car System

As early as 2008, Detroit's philanthropic and private sectors raised $125 million dollars to fund the construction of the "M-1" streetcar system, intended to link the downtown Woodward corridor to neighborhoods with development potential. However, more funds were necessary to complete the project, and fundraising prospects deteriorated as the city's economic fortunes declined.

In 2011, Detroit applied for and received a $25 million Transportation Investment Generating Economic Recovery (TIGER) grant from the Department of Transportation for the M-1 streetcar project. The Secretary of Transportation took an active interest in the project and advised stakeholders that, based on other communities' experiences, the M-1 effort was most likely to succeed if it were part of a larger regional transportation strategy. DOT staff provided technical assistance on ways to structure the M-1's finances to prevent the City from absorbing losses in the event of construction or operational cost overruns of the streetcar system.

In 2015, DOT successfully competed for a second TIGER grant of $12.2 to fund the last steps of the construction project. The Treasury Department also helped finance the construction with more than $41 million in New Market Tax Credits. Today, the streetcar system is under construction and scheduled to begin operations in April 2017.

Building Capacity for the New Regional Transportation Coordination

Before the Regional Transit Authority (RTA) was established, the various municipal and county transportation agencies coordinated service only occasionally. In general, riders must switch busses at each jurisdictional boundary. The inconvenience was compounded by Detroit's low rate of car ownership and the unusual geographic flows of its labor market: most Detroit residents (64 percent) commute out of the city for their jobs, and most Detroit jobs (74 percent) are held by non-residents. [11]

In 2011, the Secretary of Transportation advised supporters of the planned streetcar project on the importance of a larger metropolitan ridership base, a key element of the M-1's application for federal funding. In 2012, the state of Michigan passed legislation creating the RTA. In 2014, the newly-established RTA applied for and received a $6.4 million planning grant to implement a regional bus rapid transit system.

DOT staff volunteered to help the new entity prepare for its first in-depth federal review, which was scheduled to occur just two months after regular operations began. DOT provided RTA with extensive technical assistance on the procedures it would need to have in place to pass the review.

Helping Detroit Fund the "20-Minute" Neighborhood Concept

Like many American cities, until recently, much of Detroit's urban planning and development was geared towards accommodating and expediting car usage. Under the new mayor, Detroit's planning approach emphasizes the development of walkable, bike-able "20-Minute neighborhoods," in which a resident can access all of the necessities—groceries, parks, basic retail, public transit, schools —without relying on a car.

The federal team encouraged this vision of Detroit's future by making sure the City understood the publicly available funding opportunities. In 2012, the City won $10 million TIGER grant to fund non-motorized enhancements including new bike lanes and greenways. In the last few years, Detroit rebuilt its riverfront with walkways and bike-ways, including the Dequindre Cut Greenway, an urban recreational path. Formerly a Grand Trunk Railroad line, the Dequindre Cut is a predominately below-street level greenway with urban artwork and graffiti and a 20-foot-wide paved pathway for pedestrian and bicycle traffic. The two-mile greenway was developed through a public, nonprofit and private partnership comprising the federal government, City of Detroit, the Community Foundation for Southeast Michigan and the Detroit Economic Growth Corporation. In April 2016, a half-mile extension of the Dequindre Cut officially opened in the heart of Eastern Market.

---

[11] Detroiters in low-income jobs are even more likely to work outside of the city. See https://www.jpmorganchase.com/corporate/news/pr/document/csw-chase-report-untapped-talent.pdf.

Detroit aspires to extend the bikeway into a 26-mile Inner City Greenway that connects many neighborhoods with the downtown and midtown. The federal team arranged for Detroit's planning director to give a presentation on the Inner Circle Greenway at DOT headquarters. The presentation inspired one senior official to showcase Detroit's planned greenway and the "20 minute neighborhood" concept on the Transportation Secretary's Fast Lane blog.

Federal team members continue to provide technical assistance on non-motorized enhancements. At the beginning of 2016, the city had less than one mile of protected bike lanes (lanes with physical barriers protecting cyclists from vehicular traffic). By the end of this year, Detroit will have 25 miles of protected bike lanes. In addition, the city will have 212 miles of conventional bike lanes marked by painted lines, up from 63 miles in 2013.

In addition to promoting bike-ability, the city's transit strategy supports cleaner, more efficient vehicles. In 2016, DOT recognized the "Detroit-to-Chicago Zero Emission Corridor," a designation that the corridor has the infrastructure necessary for travel by electric cars.

Detroit submitted applications in grant competitions where the application planning process itself generated benefits. For example, the city applied to the highly competitive DOT Smart City Challenge Initiative, which invites cities to spell out a vision for embracing the next generation of innovative transportation technologies. Although Detroit did not win, City leaders say the application process brought public and private entities together that had not collaborated closely in the past and set in motion the City's plans to create a new Office of Mobility to coordinate Detroit's initiatives to become a hub for next-generation mobility technologies.

VI. Economic Development

At the outset of the federal team's engagement in Detroit, the City staff's energies were largely consumed by responding to short-term financial pressures and delivering basic city services. The City's economic development operations were largely administered by its quasi-public agency, the Detroit Economic Growth Corporation (DEGC).

As Detroit's circumstances have stabilized, the City has prioritized economic development: attracting and supporting businesses that provide jobs for Detroiters. In 2014, Mayor Duggan created a Jobs and Economy Team (JET) within the Mayor's Office to coordinate his economic development agenda. The federal team helped the City see the need to integrate this expanded capacity with the City's existing economic development functions. The federal team has paid particular attention to helping Detroit reestablish its manufacturing base and to developing solutions that ensure all Detroiters share in the city's recovery.

Federal Team Strategies:

- Connected the Mayor's JET team and the DEGC to Economic Development Administration (EDA) experts who could explain how to remedy gaps in grant proposals.

- Answered the City's request for assistance with reindustrialization plans.

- Adapted new ways to use HUD CDBG funds to support entrepreneurial development.

- Educated civic leaders, coalitions and community organizations about publicly-announced opportunities to apply for various federal resources for manufacturing communities and research facilities.

- Ensured that non-profit organization serving minority entrepreneurs was aware of the funding opportunity for a Minority Business Development Center

- Partnered with national, Michigan-based philanthropy and two non-profits to launch initiative providing entrepreneurship education and microloans to citizens returning from incarceration.

Resources to Help Detroit Revitalize an Industrial Corridor

In 2012, the City identified the Mt. Elliott Industrial Corridor as having high potential for increased manufacturing activity. Redevelopment of this neighborhood was a centerpiece of a larger strategy to attract industry and automotive manufacturing back to Detroit proper.

The City engaged the DFWG, which helped it search for potential federal funding opportunities. In 2014, the City put together a winning proposal for a $600,000 EDA grant to fund an assessment of the industrial corridor's development potential. Equipped with this assessment, in 2016, the City persuaded an automotive supplier to locate its new $95 million manufacturing plant in the corridor.

The federal team used the assessment as it looked for ways to help the City sustain momentum in the industrial corridor. The DFWG helped the City understand how federal funds could be integrated into corridor strategy, and the City put together a successful proposal for a $3.2 million EDA grant to for infrastructure improvements in the industrial corridor. The EDA opportunity provides an example of how a planning grant can lay the groundwork for an eventual implementation grant.

Helping City Build out Economic Development Team

The Mayor approached the federal team about ways to increase the City's economic development staffing. The DFWG helped the Mayor's office identify federal grant opportunities and worked with the City to address potential gaps in its grant proposals.

In 2016, the City successfully applied for a $910,000 EDA grant to fund an Economic Recovery Coordination team, housed at DEGC and operated in coordination with the Mayor's JET team. The Economic Recovery Coordination team will manage and execute all elements of Detroit's re-industrialization efforts, including business attraction and site identification. The City estimates this increased staff will help it attract or create 5,000 new jobs to Detroit over a five-year period.

Two New Manufacturing Research Facility Investments

In 2015 and 2016, the DFWG informed Detroit leaders about opportunities to attract federally-supported research facilities through the National Network of Manufacturing Institutes (NNMI Institutes). The federal team could not provide technical assistance to applicants in either of these competitions because they were solicitations for cooperative agreements.

Detroit proposals succeeded both times. Detroit was the only city in the country to attract two NNMI Institutes:

- *Advanced Composites Manufacturing Innovation* (IACMI), funded by the Department of Energy: Researchers at IACMI work to develop lower-cost, higher-speed, and more efficient manufacturing and recycling processes for advanced composites.

- *Lightweight Innovations for Tomorrow* (LIFT), funded by the Department of the Navy: LIFT will speed the development of new lightweight metal manufacturing processes from laboratories to factories.

The two research facilities focus on complementary technologies and are co-located—in Detroit's oldest neighborhood—to facilitate collaboration on automotive research applications.

Motor City Match: Business Competition for Businesses and Commercial Space

In 2015, the DEGC approached HUD with a proposal for a Motor City Match program with two strategies: a quarterly competition for small businesses and for commercial property owners. The program includes matchmaking to connect the businesses with Detroit real estate opportunities. In Motor City Match, small businesses receive free business planning classes and other technical support. Building owners receive architectural design services and introductions to businesses looking for space to rent.

DEGC wanted to know whether HUD Community Development Block Grants (CDBG) could be used to fund the awards. Although CDBG funds had not historically been used in this way, HUD and the DFWG worked closely with the City to ensure compliance with HUD regulations.

Since its launch in 2015, Motor City Match has committed over $2.9 million in CDBG funds to assist 40 local businesses and property owners. In addition to the CDBG funds, philanthropic foundations have pledged an additional $2 million to the program, creating a successful public/private partnership. To date, the program has supported 385 businesses with technical assistance and grants: Of these, 72 percent are minority-owned, 68 percent are women-owned, and 52 percent are minority-women owned.

Targeted Assistance for Minority Entrepreneurs and Manufacturers

The federal team and the City recognize inclusivity as a pillar of effective, meaningful economic development. The DFWG provided the City with assistance in developing strategies that address the needs of traditionally-underserved communities.

In 2016, the Department of Commerce's Minority Business Development Agency (MBDA) announced a competition for grants to support minority business development centers. These centers provide minority-owned businesses with technical assistance, business introductions and networking opportunities. The centers will help any company identify opportunities to include minority-owned businesses among its suppliers. The DFWG helped ensure that the public grant announcement reached Detroit's economic development organizations.

The Michigan Minority Supplier Development Council (MMSDC), which operated the existing minority business development center in Detroit, re-competed for assistance and was awarded $1.55 million to over five years. In November 2016, the MMSDC won a second competitive grant from the MBDA: $1.25 million over five years to fund technical assistance and business development services for minority-owned businesses in the advanced manufacturing sector.

In February 2016, Detroit's own independent My Brother's Keeper team launched the "Innovation Challenge" which will invest $500,000 in crowdsourced ideas that enable young men of color to connect to the city's emerging Information Age economy.[12]

Federal Competition Inspires Coalition to Form and Devise Manufacturing Strategy for Detroit Region

In 2012, the federal team ensured that Detroit audiences were included in the national publicity efforts for the Investing in Manufacturing Communities Partnership (IMCP), an inter-agency competition hosted by the EDA for coalitions representing manufacturing regions. Each competing coalition submitted a comprehensive economic development strategy to "strengthen [the region's] competitive edge for attracting manufacturer and supply-chain investments." Winning regions were designated "IMCP Manufacturing Communities" and received preference in applications for certain future federal programs.

Over thirty organizations in the Greater Detroit region formed the IMCP-awarded *Advance Michigan* coalition, focused on automotive manufacturing and research. *Advance Michigan* was the first super-regional collaboration among Southeastern Michigan's local governments, economic developers, nonprofits, organized labor, research universities, community colleges and federally-funded research/investment centers. The coalition's proposal included commitments from non-federal sources for $177 million in private sector workforce development training.

---

[12] This competition was made possible by a partnership between the Skillman Foundation and the Campaign for Black Male Achievement.

Advance Michigan-associated applicants received preference points that contributed to their winning $33 million in federal funding awards over two years. After its initial two-year designation expired, *Advance Michigan* received a two-year extension of its IMCP status.

Partnering to Provide Entrepreneurial Opportunities for Formerly-Incarcerated Detroiters

In 2015, the U.S. Small Business Administration (SBA) began discussions with the W.K. Kellogg Foundation and the micro-lending organization Justine Petersen to create a pilot initiative—"ASPIRE"—that provides entrepreneurship education and microloans to formerly-incarcerated individuals. Many returning citizens are unable to secure jobs upon their release and therefore fail to meet their child-support obligations. The ASPIRE initiative will create new pathways to financial education and potential income.

One of the SBA leads on this initiative was an agency representative to the DFWG. Aware that approximately 3,000 Detroiters return to the city from incarceration every year, the SBA lead coordinated with the DFWG to position Detroit as one of the first cities selected by the W.K. Kellogg Foundation for the pilot. The ASPIRE initiative's launch was announced in Detroit in August of 2016. The SBA lead has since worked with other DFWG members to locate additional non-profits to serve as implementation partners.

VII.   International Affairs

"[A]t the State Department, we understand the very valuable role that cities can play in addressing a wide range of challenges. And that is why we're working directly with cities like Detroit, which is opening up its first-ever Office of International Affairs."
                                                                    – U.S. Secretary of State Kerry

As a prominent international border city with an iconic international cultural legacy, global industry, port and a large foreign-born population in the region, Detroit is well-positioned for international engagement. Canada is the United States' largest trading partner, and the Detroit-Windsor border is the second richest border crossing in the country.[13] The Detroit area is home to the largest concentration of Arab people outside of the Middle East.

However, until recently, the need to respond to the local economic crisis hindered Detroit from planning, executing, and staffing a concerted global engagement strategy. As a result, Detroit has lacked capacity in the area of international affairs. In contrast to peer cities, Detroit lacked an office of international affairs, international adviser, and an international business attraction office within its economic development agency. The City also lacked staff capacity for addressing immigrant affairs.

In keeping with its efforts to help build the City's long-term capacity, the DFWG has helped Detroit develop an international engagement strategy that the City can build on to advance its recovery, rehabilitate its global "brand," and position Detroit for future success.

Federal Team Strategies

- Convened discussions with Detroit leaders and federal agencies to design a global engagement strategy and a long-term international affairs structure and resources for Detroit.

- Provided protocol services and coordination for the Mayor. Met with consular offices and visiting international delegations, represented the Mayor at international events, spoke regularly to visiting professional exchange groups.

- Initiated a planning process, led by City officials, to review how immigrants are resettled in Detroit and what support services, such as housing, employment, health, transportation, and schools, can be provided to facilitate their resettlement.

- Facilitated meetings for the Mayor with senior US government agency leaders so that he could present his plans for resettling immigrants and refugees in Detroit.

- Provided technical assistance for structuring trade delegations and for using global partnerships and exports to create jobs and benefits for Detroiters.

- Initiated a review of underleveraged global infrastructure and untapped economic opportunities in Detroit, such as international waterways and the port.

- Helped Detroit leaders showcase the city as a dynamic and welcoming place for entrepreneurs and growing businesses.

---

[13] The Detroit-Windsor border crossing exchanges over $350 in bilateral trade per day, making it the second richest border crossing in the country after Laredo, Texas.

Creating Detroit's First Global Engagement Strategy

The DFWG is helping Detroit develop its first strategy to leverage global engagement that supports Detroit's recovery. This strategy includes a plan for the City to communicate the value of international engagement to Detroiters and a structure for business and civic leaders to coordinate on global affairs.

To develop this strategy, the DFWG held group meetings with federal agencies (State Department, Customs and Border Protection, Department of Commerce, Small Business Administration, EXIM Bank). Separately, the DFWG met individually with foundations, chambers of commerce, trade groups, consulates, business leaders, national and international partners, local stakeholders and City staff. The DFWG also met individually with prominent global organizations, such as The German Marshall Fund of the United States and The Kresge Foundation, to develop the non-governmental elements of the strategy. The strategy was informed by the work of global leaders such as JP Morgan Chase and the Brookings Institution on Global Cities; the Council on Foreign Relations (CFR); and The Africa Center in New York.

The DFWG convened over twenty federal agencies to offer recommendations to the Mayor on how the federal government could partner with Detroit on a global engagement strategy. This process included cataloguing existing federal resources for city-level international engagement, future technical assistance and capacity-building options, assessing assets such as Detroit's port, cross-border trade and others.

The DFWG efforts benefitted from ideas and resources from the Office of the Secretary at the State Department, notably through the Cities@State initiative. The Secretary of State launched this effort in October 2015, with the attendance of Detroit Mayor Duggan. This subnational diplomacy initiative connects global mayors and City leaders to promote sharing of innovative thinking about global challenges. Through this State Department platform, the DFWG coordinated with numerous US embassies, and domestic and global city offices of international affairs.

Resettling Refugees: Providing Strategic Advice and Building a Coalition

Shortly after the DFWG began its work in Detroit, the Administration announced its commitment to a significant increase in U.S refugee resettlement from Syria. The State Department worked with local resettlement agencies across the country to determine the best candidate cities for increasing refugee populations. Starting in August 2015, the DFWG began working closely with the US Permanent Representative to the United Nations, senior leadership at the State Department and the Bureau of Population, Refugees and Migration (PRM), and senior leadership at several federal agencies to build a strategy for refugee resettlement from all nations in Detroit.

The DFWG suggested to the Mayor that City officials meet with resettlement agencies across the metro region to obtain feedback on past efforts and to determine capacity in Detroit. The DFWG and the City convened a working group of stakeholders to draft the resettlement strategy that would be coordinated by the City's new head of Immigrant Affairs.

The DFWG cultivated relationships with senior officials at the State Department Bureau of Population, Refugee and Migration for guidance on the refugee process. As a result, the Mayor was able to meet with the U.S. Permanent Representative to the United Nations, the National Economic Council Director, the OMB Director, the Domestic Policy Council Director, the National Security Council staff, and senior leadership at HUD, HHS, and DHS in support of this strategy.

In 2015, in consultation with the DFWG, the City officials drafted the first Detroit Refugee Resettlement Strategy, which was presented to the State Department. The strategy included a "Detroit innovation" to the refugee process in Detroit— an initiative with HUD to rehabilitate housing for both refugees and Detroiters.

In October 2015, the resettlement agencies, City agencies, and community partners agreed to form a *Detroit Refugee Resettlement Working Group* to develop and execute a plan with clear goals for refugee resettlement in Detroit. This working group continues to meet with the City's Director of Immigrant Affairs to realize the Mayor's goal of resettling and retaining 50 new refugee families per year in Detroit. At the time of this report, more than 40 refugee families, totaling over 300 individuals, were re-settled successfully in Detroit in 2016.

Capacity Building and Technical Assistance for International Trade Missions and Exports

The DFWG has worked to help connect Detroit's leadership and businesses to global opportunities by building capacity for effective trade missions and by developing a job-focused export strategy.

- Japan: The DFWG provided staff capacity and technical assistance in executing the Mayor's first international mission. The DFWG advised the Mayor on the economic opportunity for Detroit in the Japanese market, resulting in an extended trip by the Mayor with Detroit companies to participate in high-level economic meetings supported by the U.S. Embassy. In support of Detroit's food sector, the Foreign Agriculture Office arranged meetings with Japanese food industry leaders. The Embassy Energy attaché arranged meetings with energy sector leaders. The Foreign Commercial Service Chief arranged meetings with potential partners in advanced manufacturing, education, and the creative sectors. The DFWG worked with the embassy to secure a meeting for the Mayor with the top economic official at the Ministry of Foreign Affairs.

- Europe: The DFWG structured a staff mission to Italy in fall 2016 in collaboration with the US Consulate in Milan showcasing Detroit's creative sectors. At the Venice Biennale[14], the State Department's American Pavilion focused on Detroit's architectural legacy, the only exhibition on an individual city. The US Consulate in Milan arranged for City leaders to present at the American Pavilion, and arranged meetings at the UNESCO City of Design office, with City of Venice leaders, and with the President of the Venice Biennale. The group proceeded to participate in the City of Bilbao's BUILD conference on urban innovation, met with City leaders, and visited adaptive reuse cultural spaces.

- China: The DFWG provided technical assistance to the Mayor in cooperation with the US Embassy in China for a trade mission led by the Governor of Michigan. The DFWG coordinated with the Governor's staff on visits to Detroit by senior Chinese officials and helped develop an MOU proposal for an economic partnership between Detroit and the City of Shenzhen, known as the "Silicon Valley" of China.

---

[14] The Venice Biennale, established in 1895, is one of the oldest and most prestigious art events in the world, welcoming hundreds of thousands of visitors a year --significant positive exposure for the City of Detroit.

- <u>Cuba:</u> The DFWG worked with the US Charge d'Affaires in Havana to organize a fact-finding mission for the Mayor's Jobs and Economy Chief.

- <u>Algeria:</u> The DFWG looked for opportunities to incorporate diaspora partnerships in the global engagement strategy, for example in Africa. The DFWG helped Detroit host the largest private sector delegation from Algeria ever to visit the United States, including more than 60 CEOs, the Algerian Ambassador to the United States and the U.S. Ambassador to Algeria.

Finally, the DFWG worked to include export strategies that link federal and local efforts in the broader global engagement strategy design. DFWG asked SBA, the Department of Commerce, and EXIM Bank to inventory export-ready companies in strategic sectors such as food, mobility, advanced manufacturing and the creative sectors. The DFWG asked agencies to compile Detroit-specific data on jobs supported by exports, catalogue best practices for outcome-oriented trade missions, and developed recommendations for export promotion. [15]

Capacity Building around Entrepreneurship

Another Mayoral priority is fostering the entrepreneurial culture in Detroit. The DFWG partnered with a leading foundation in Detroit, the New Economy Initiative (NEI), to feature Detroit on the global entrepreneurship stage at the President's *Global Entrepreneurship Summit* (GES) in Silicon Valley. GES 2016 brought together 1,200 entrepreneurs and investors from 170 countries. The event featured sessions addressing challenges to entrepreneurship and opportunities for showcasing successes. Through DFWG' efforts, Detroit was represented by several official entrepreneur delegates, and held the only city-specific partner event at GES. The Detroit Story @ GES featured 15 leading Detroit innovators and entrepreneurs chosen to feature Detroit's entrepreneurial culture.

The DFWG highlighted Detroit's status as an global emerging market for civic entrepreneurship and innovation at White House events such as South x South Lawn, and worked with the State Department to launch a Detroit-based micro-granting model called Detroit Soup in two cities in Tunisia at the 2015 U.S. – Tunisia Entrepreneurship and Investment Conference with the U.S. Secretary of Commerce. Detroit Soup provides a platform for funding social entrepreneurship projects through small donations at community dinners where winners are selected based on a democratic vote.[16]

Global Branding/Public Diplomacy

DFWG has also helped put Detroit back on the global map by engaging with international partners and the State Department on a communications strategy for repositioning Detroit on a global stage. The DFWG helped the City navigate successfully the State Department's nomination process for the UNESCO City of Design designation. Detroit is now the only American city to achieve this international designation within the prestigious UNESCO Creative Cities Network. Recognizing the significance of this designation, the DFWG organized a study tour to Europe in October 2016 focused on UNESCO Cities of Design. In line with the State Department's Cities@State initiative, the State Department highlighted Detroit, at the 2016 Architectural Biennale, the first time the American Pavilion focused on a city.

---

[15] For example, DFWG worked to incorporate State Department best practices for economic engagement, such as the Bureau of Economic and Business Affairs (EB) Direct Line model for encouraging businesses to export and invest in strategic markets

[16] The White House identified Detroit Soup as a "Champion of Change." Detroit Soup has funded over 45 projects in Detroit, 39 non-profits, and 25 for-profit enterprises. It conducted Soups in Europe, Tunisia, and Nepal.

VIII. Policing & Public Safety

For decades, Detroit has been challenged by violent crime, and effective policing has been hindered by insufficient resources and fraught community relationships. By 2003, the situation deteriorated to the point that the Department of Justice (DOJ) entered into a consent decree with the City and the Detroit Police Department (DPD) to reform its policing and detention practices. The City's economic struggles and eventual bankruptcy created further stresses for public safety efforts, so there was no shortage of need when DOJ began its focused effort to assist Detroit.

With DOJ's active support, DPD's efforts appear to be yielding promising results: the number of homicides has decreased every year since 2012.

Federal Team Strategies

- Assisted DPD's reform of policing practices and detention conditions to meet the requirements of its consent decree.

- Connected the City to DOJ's Violence Reduction Network, an initiative to address local priorities with all of DOJ's component resources and a peer network for exchanging best practices and education.

- Partnered with Michigan State University to develop a program to train crime data analysts, freeing up the DPD officers who previously conducted crime analytics for assignments enforcing public safety and advancing community policing.

- Convened police, prosecutors' offices and community members in a "Ceasefire" partnership to reduce youth violence by targeting known violent gang members.

- Linked Detroit to the White House Police Data Initiative, a peer learning network of cities that publish policing data on the internet to promote public engagement and trust and to guide policing decisions.

Helping Detroit Meet the Conditions of the Civil Rights Consent Decree

In 2003, following DOJ's two-and-a-half-year investigation into the DPD's use of force, the City entered into a consent judgment that required comprehensive reforms to remedy DPD's patterns and practices of excessive force and unlawful detentions and arrests. A second consent judgment addressed unconstitutional conditions of confinement in the DPD's holding cells.

As part of the remedy process, DOJ's Civil Rights Division, the U.S. Attorney's Office for the Eastern District of Michigan and the City worked cooperatively throughout the duration of the settlement. Although there was not always agreement among the parties, all participants put forth the sustained effort needed to achieve constitutional policing practices. Ultimately, the Detroit Police Department eliminated the unconstitutional practices that made the consent judgment necessary through comprehensive policy revision; enhanced training, supervision and investigative practices; and improved accountability systems, including a comprehensive risk management system. The effects of these changes are evident in fewer officer-involved shootings and other uses of force, and the abolition of DPD's past practice of detaining witnesses during investigations of serious crimes.

In August 2014, the Justice Department announced the termination of the consent judgment relating to the use of force and arrest and witness detention practices.[17] Notably, DOJ and the City of Detroit jointly sought the approval of a Transition Agreement maintaining federal oversight for an additional 18 months, concluding February 2016. The transition agreement signaled a new chapter of reform and accountability as it represented DPD's ongoing commitment to ensure constitutional policing, promote community confidence, and improve public safety.

Using DOJ's Violence Reduction Network to Access Resources and Learn Best Practices

The primary violence reduction collaboration between the City and the federal government has been the DOJ's Violence Reduction Network (VRN). Detroit joined the VRN as an inaugural member in 2014. The VRN is a comprehensive violence reduction strategy to deploy the spectrum of DOJ resources, both program and law enforcement, in a customized training and technical assistance effort. VRN supports rather than supplants a jurisdiction's existing violent crime strategies.

Through VRN, DOJ provided Detroit expedited access to resources and subject-matter experts to review strengths, promising programs and developments, and identify gaps, unmet needs, and areas for improvement. The specific areas in which DPD indicated critical resource needs to address violence were: (1) youth, gang and drug-related violence; (2) technology support / assessments; (3) homicide reduction; and (4) effective grant strategies.

A notable outcome of Detroit's participation in VRN is the increased collaboration and information-sharing among local and federal agency partners. The DPD, the Wayne County Prosecutor's Office, the Michigan Department of Corrections, and the Michigan State Police share information about current activities and initiatives during biweekly VRN conference calls.

VRN connected the DPD with the Federal Bureau of Investigation's digital program to display fugitives' photos on billboards. The first Detroit offender was posted on the digital billboards in August 2015. The DPD is connected with an FBI contact, allowing the DPD to provide new offender information as necessary. VRN also supplemented the solid work of Detroit's public safety agencies with technical assistance from DOJ's law enforcement agencies. A FBI Violent Crime Coordinator facilitates FBI resources to focus on street gangs and drug-related violence. The FBI supported overtime costs for DPD officers through this initiative. Additionally, the Bureau of Alcohol, Tobacco and Firearms embedded three agents in the DPD homicide unit to improve investigative capacity. Similarly, the Drug Enforcement Agency and the U.S. Marshal's Service partnered with Detroit area law enforcement agencies to conduct a multi-jurisdictional drug trafficking operation and fugitive apprehension operations in 2015.

DOJ's Detroit Public Safety Partners
• U.S. Attorney's Office, Eastern District of Michigan
• Detroit Police Department
• Wayne County Prosecutor's Office
• Detroit Mayor's Office
• Detroit Public Schools Police Department
• Michigan State Police
• Michigan Department of Corrections
• Michigan State University

In 2014, the DOJ provided the DPD with a technology assessment and recommendations, which led to specific improvements in DPD's warrant automation process.

---

[17]The other concurrent consent judgment relating to the conditions of confinement in DPD holding cells was terminated in early 2014 after the City fully complied with that judgment's terms and transferred custodial responsibility for all DPD detainees to the Michigan Department of Corrections.

To address domestic violence homicides, VRN assisted the Detroit partners to implement a Domestic Violence Fatality Review Board. The Board reviews domestic violence-related deaths to prevent future incidents, preserve the safety of battered women, and hold accountable the perpetrators and the Detroit and Wayne County agencies and organizations that come into contact with the parties.

To strengthen the Detroit PD's grant-seeking capabilities, DOJ coordinated specialized technical assistance with nationally recognized experts to help the DPD establish a grants committee and a grants strategic plan. As a result, Detroit developed the infrastructure to support a coordinated approach to grant seeking. Following VRN grant writing and development training, in fiscal year 2015 Detroit competed successfully for more than $6.5 million in DOJ grants related to body-worn cameras, testing sexual assault kits, adopting technology innovation, DPD staffing, addressing human trafficking, and addressing arrest policies and enforcement of protection orders.

Developing a Program to Train Data-Driven Crime Analysts

To support Detroit's crime-fighting capability, VRN connected the Detroit agencies and Michigan State University (MSU) to develop a crime analyst program. Prior to this project, DPD officers who had minimal training in crime analysis conducted crime analysis. This staff assignment resulted in less effective analysis and prevented those officers from engaging in critical public safety and patrol activities. Under the new program, graduate students from the MSU master's program in law enforcement, intelligence and analysis are embedded in the DPD, the Wayne County Prosecutor's Office, and the Detroit Public Schools Police Department. These students support proactive, data-driven crime prevention and control. In addition to building the analytic capacity within the agencies, the MSU project fostered a common understanding of how data should inform policing strategy.

Reducing Youth Violence with "Ceasefire," a Community-Led Partnership

To address youth violence, Detroit initiated the "Ceasefire Model." Ceasefire is a community-led program enforced by a partnership among federal, state and local law enforcement agencies and the affected communities to reduce homicide and violent crime.

The Ceasefire Model suppresses gun violence by focusing on defusing the rivalries between small groups of high-rate offenders, such as gangs and drug crews, who perpetrate most street violence. Ceasefire Detroit rapidly responds to shootings with actions directed toward the group and its associates who are identified through social network analysis. The Ceasefire team also coordinates services for shooting victims, beginning at the hospital.

As a result of sustained focus by the Mayor and Police Chief, Detroit is making steady progress in engaging youth. DOJ believes that the key to success of the efforts begin with the fact that DPD, community and public safety stakeholders are willing partners. Critically, DOJ did not impose change on DPD, but rather proactively engaged the City in developing the solutions to problems it knows the most about. DOJ encouraged open and free dialogue about what worked and what didn't. Finally, success depended on the leadership of the Attorney General and the commitment of DOJ's component agencies.

Police Data Initiative: Publishing Data on the Internet for Evidence-Based Decision-Making

The White House Police Data Initiative (PDI) is a nationwide community of practice of law enforcement agencies across the country. Under PDI, law enforcement agencies commit to publish at least three data sets about policing to increase transparency and accountability with the community. Jurisdictions choose which data sets they will release based on local priorities, and they determine their own timelines for data release, based on their capacity and the condition of their data.

The most important element to success in PDI is leadership buy-in. Detroit's mayor had launched an open data initiative in February 2015, and as the City entered its post-consent decree era, the police chief reiterated that transparency was a top priority. For the DPD, open data provided an opportunity to make a long-term shift from federal government oversight to community oversight. The police department has a strong citizen advisory board that was well-positioned to advise on which data sets were released and how to present them to the public in a useful way.

Nationwide, municipal police departments often lag in adopting open data initiatives. However, Detroit's police department is setting an example for its own city in data transparency, inspiring other departments such as code enforcement and public works to follow suit. In the same way, the peer PDI agencies across the country motivate DPD to move their police data transparency to the next level.

Peer-to-peer learning occurs in biweekly phone calls with roll-call-style reports from each agency on progress toward opening data and barriers. City of Detroit staff report that the regular cadence of sharing best practices with other jurisdictions has built their own internal capacity. This format normalized the internal struggles that even high-capacity jurisdictions can face, and allows cities like Detroit to share their local innovations in a leadership role.

PDI has deepened the partnership between the police department and IT departments. Most importantly, Detroit's work on the PDI has spurred a shift in organizational culture that extends into other initiatives. The presumption now is that data should be public, and program staff look for opportunities to open data to build trust and align public-private efforts.

IX.   Observations from Detroit: Key Lessons and the Path Forward

The federal government responded to the extraordinary economic and civic crisis in Detroit with an unusual assignment of full-time staff from Washington, DC and regional offices, as well as creating a working group of over 20 federal agencies. This degree of engagement between federal and local government would be difficult to implement widely. Nonetheless, the Detroit experience involved dynamics and issues that other federal-local collaborations would confront in any number of places and circumstances.

- **Strong local leadership can amplify impact.** The Mayor's enthusiastic support for and active commitment to the federal-local partnership helped the team get traction and maintain momentum.

- **Philanthropic partnerships can help advance ambitious projects.** Detroit's philanthropic community brought flexible resources, local knowledge, and additional convening power to the federal-local partnership.

- **Alignment with local priorities is critical.** The Mayor directed the core team's attention toward areas he deemed the highest priority, so that the DFWG could work in tandem with City staff. The mayor's priorities were informed by numerous civic planning efforts, for example, the Detroit Future City plan. In some cases, the federal team brought new ideas to the Mayor's attention.

- **The team's White House affiliation and status as an Administration priority increases its effectiveness.** The White House affiliation lends credibility within the Administration and with city stakeholders. This affiliation substantially boosted the team's convening power.

- **Staying knowledgeable of fast-changing local conditions:** Since 2011, local conditions changed quickly in Detroit: the city experienced municipal bankruptcy and financial control by an emergency manager; the influx of millions of dollars of philanthropic and business investment; and the election of a new Mayor. To stay current on these developments, the assigned staff of DFWG communicated daily. The all-agency Working Group met monthly with Detroit speakers and circulated written updates.

- **Ideally, federal staff are empowered to navigate the federal agency structure and use their knowledge of agency resources.**

- **The federal team should set clear expectations with the City about the role of federal team as builders of capacity ("co-creators of solutions").** The federal team embedded with City staff, but remained independent with responsibilities as members of the federal service.

The Path Forward

The federal engagement in Detroit presents a case study for the Community Solutions approach to federal-local collaboration: over the years, the collaboration took different organizational forms, involved multiple agencies and addressed a wide variety of community needs and priorities.

This report strives to capture many of the lessons of this engagement for future federal initiatives and surface some best practices that could be used by other communities.

The progress made in Detroit is an endorsement of the Community Solutions approach. Along a number of dimensions, Detroit is better-positioned than it was when the federal engagement began, and Detroit has vastly greater capacity to partner with federal, state, public and private entities.

X.   Recent Federal Commitments to Detroit

The examples below illustrate the depth, breadth and diversity of the sustained federal commitment to Detroit, focusing on the period from Detroit's bankruptcy in 2013 to the present. These investments of funding, expertise and attention are organized by federal agency, with combined initiatives listed at the end.

YEAR	AGENCY/ EXECUTIVE OFFICE	DESCRIPTION
2015-2017	U.S. Department of Agriculture – Food and Nutrition Service	**Job Counseling for Detroiters Getting Food Assistance**: The Detroit Supplemental Nutrition Assistance Program - Employment and Training (SNAP E&T) initiative provides job-driven training to up to 200 participants and then connects them to job vacancies.
2014-2016	U.S. Department of Agriculture – Food and Nutrition Service	**Pilot to Provide Summer Food Security for Detroit Youth:** In 2013 Detroit was selected for USDA's Summer Electronic Benefits Transfer (SEBT) for Children pilot. Each year, K-12 Detroit Public School students who qualify for free or reduced price school meals receive an EBT card with funds for food purchases over the summer months, significantly reducing food insecurity and improving nutrition. The benefits can be redeemed at 576 authorized vendors in Detroit and Wayne County. The pilot has grown substantially: in 2013, over 12,000 Detroit Public School students participated; in 2016, over 37,000 students participated.
2011-2014	U.S. Department of Agriculture – Forest Service	**Outdoor Environmental Education for Detroit Students**: The Forest Service awarded an $82K grant to Michigan Technological University to develop a Forest Stewardship education program for inner-city Detroit teachers and to assist them in integrating natural resources into their curriculum. Approximately 60 teachers were trained, reaching more than 1,800 Detroit and Wayne County students in Grades 5-12.
2010-2016	U.S. Department of Agriculture – Forest Service	**Planting and Protecting Trees in Detroit:** The Forest Service has provided nearly $3 million in grants to the non-profit The Greening of Detroit to restore damaged tree canopy and remove toxins from vacant lots. More than 9,000 trees have been planted in Detroit. In cooperation with the Michigan Department of Natural Resources-Forestry, the Forest Service awarded over $800K to inventory Detroit's trees, which helped Detroit remove dead trees for public safety.
2016	Department of Commerce – Economic Development Administration	**Continuing Industrial Corridor's Momentum with $3.2 million for Infrastructure:** Detroit earned a $3.2 million EDA grant to fund the redevelopment and expansion of Georgia Street, part of the Mt. Elliot Industrial Corridor. The projects funded were identified as strategic priorities in the 2014 corridor study, also funded by EDA. This second

YEAR	AGENCY/ EXECUTIVE OFFICE	DESCRIPTION
		EDA investment is projected to generate over 600 new jobs and $120 million in private investment.
2016	Department of Commerce – Economic Development Administration	**Funding an Economic Recovery Team to Help Detroit Compete for Business:** EDA awarded $910K to fund the hiring of an Economic Recovery Coordination Team for the City. The team will oversee Detroit's re-industrialization efforts, including business attraction and identifying sites for development. The City estimates this staff capacity will help create 5,000 new jobs in Detroit over five years.
2014- Present	Department of Commerce – Economic Development Administration	**EDA Supports the Creation of Blueprint for Revitalized Mount Elliot Corridor:** In 2014, EDA awarded Detroit a $600K grant for a corridor study of the Mount Elliott Employment District that identified infrastructure improvements that could draw new or expanding businesses to the industrial neighborhood.
2012- Present	Department of Commerce – Economic Development Administration	**Developing a Comprehensive Regional Plan for Spurring Manufacturing:** Detroit was one of the first 12 communities to receive the "Manufacturing Community" designation from the "Investing in Manufacturing Community Partnership (IMCP)," a federal, inter-agency initiative to support comprehensive, community-designed economic development strategies. The *Advance Michigan* consortium of over 30 organizations partnered to develop a strategy to enhance the Detroit region's automotive technology and manufacturing capabilities with new supplier networks, infrastructure, export and foreign direct investment opportunities. The IMCP Manufacturing Community designation prompted *Advance Michigan* and its partners to commit to $177 million for training and workforce development activities.
2016	Department of Commerce – Minority Business Development Agency	**Business Development Resources for Minority Entrepreneurs and Manufacturers:** The Michigan Minority Supplier Development Council (MMSDC) successfully re-competed for a five-year grant totaling $1.55 million to fund its minority business development center. In November 2016, the MMSDC won a second competitive grant: $1.25 million over five years to fund technical assistance and business development services to minority-owned advanced manufacturing businesses.
2014	Department of Defense	**Groundbreaking Auto Parts Research through Manufacturing Innovation Hubs:** In 2014, Detroit won the competition for the Department of Defense's Lightweight Innovations for Tomorrow (LIFT) lab, bringing over $140 million in public-private investment in cutting-edge manufacturing research to Detroit's oldest neighborhood, Corktown. The lightweight materials research has applications for

YEAR	AGENCY/ EXECUTIVE OFFICE	DESCRIPTION
		automotive research and is complemented by the 2015 co-location of the IACMI composites research facility.
2013-2016	Department of Energy	**Provided Technical Assistance Enabling City to Replace Failing Street Light Infrastructure with City High-Efficiency Lighting:** DOE provided technical assistance on advanced lighting to the newly established Public Lighting Authority (PLA). In less than two years, the city will go from being in majority darkness to being re-lit with a smaller carbon footprint. Early estimates show that the light-emitting diode (LED) street lights will save nearly 46 million kilowatts of energy per year, resulting in nearly $3 million in annual cost savings for the City. Anticipated emissions reductions are equivalent to the annual emissions from 10,993 passenger vehicles.
2012-2016	Department of Energy	**DOE Technical Assistance Helps Transform Closed Park into Urban Solar Facility:** The Department of Energy provided technical assistance to help the City and local electric utility, DTE Energy, convert the decommissioned O'Shea Park into a pioneering 10-acre solar array. The solar facility will open in early summer 2017 and will generate electricity valued at $125K annually.
2016	Department of Energy	**MOU Lays Groundwork for Partnership with Argonne National Lab:** The DFWG explored whether Detroit and Argonne would be interested in a partnership whereby Argonne will provide its expertise in transportation, infrastructure and sustainability analysis to the City and support its plans to create a Chief Mobility Office. The parties signed an MOU in September 2016.
2015	Department of Energy	**The Institute for Advanced Composites Manufacturing Innovation co-locates research operations with LIFT.** Advanced composite and lightweight material research both have applications for automotive manufacturing; co-location facilitates research that integrates both kinds of technology.
2014-2016	Department of Energy and the Environmental Protection Agency	**Supporting City's Creation of Sustainability Office:** The agencies have helped the City determine staffing strategy, priorities and work plan for the office, planned to open in 2017. The office will address interdepartmental projects such as green infrastructure, energy efficiency, and greening the municipal fleet of vehicles.

YEAR	AGENCY/ EXECUTIVE OFFICE	DESCRIPTION
2016-2017	Environmental Protection Agency and Department of Interior-National Park Service	**Accelerated Timing of Planned Riverfront Park Investments by Five years to Align with City's Parks Masterplan:** The City's new park improvement masterplan outlines the city's planned investments in park infrastructure. Reviewing the plan, the EPA and NPS realized that federal investments planned for 2021 would have greater impact if synchronized with the city-funded improvements. The federal team was able to accelerate the investments and, consequently, city investments in three upper riverfront parks (AB Ford, Lakefront East, and Mariner Park) will be matched with EPA Great Lakes Restoration Initiative funding and National Park Service Rivers and Trails technical assistance.
2013-2016	Environmental Protection Agency	**Provide Technical Assistance on Better Blight Elimination:** EPA developed a residential demolition bid specification toolkit in 2013, which allowed the City to review a menu of environmentally-sensitive activities associated with residential building removal. EPA and Michigan Department of Environmental Quality staff continue to work regularly with the Detroit Building Authority on materials management, asbestos, fugitive dust, brownfields, environmental justice, and storm-water management.
2015	Environmental Protection Agency	**Replacing Old Diesel Trucks with Newer, Cleaner Ones:** EPA awarded a $1 million grant that enabled a local non-governmental organization (Southwest Detroit Environmental Vision) to replace the high-emission, older vehicles used to haul materials from the port with new, greener diesel trucks.
2014	Environmental Protection Agency	**Constructing Green Infrastructure on Vacant Lots:** EPA awarded $1 million Great Lake Restoration Initiative Shoreline Cities grant to construct green infrastructure projects on the lower eastside of Detroit. Construction is underway with Detroit foundations and job training non-profits as an initial conservation corps project.
2014	Environmental Protection Agency	**Brownfield Assessment and Revolving Loan Fund for Brownfield Clean-up:** Brownfield grant funds ($600K for assessment and $1.7 million for revolving loan fund) enable site redevelopment by financing the assessment, clean up, and infrastructure improvements needed to rehabilitate brownfield sites.
2014	Environmental Protection Agency	**Local and National Experts Brought Together for Green Demolition Workshop:** EPA convened a workshop of experts for focused discussions on ways to incorporate materials management, health, and workforce development strategies into planned residential demolitions.

YEAR	AGENCY/ EXECUTIVE OFFICE	DESCRIPTION
2016	Environmental Protection Agency and Department of Justice	**EPA and DOJ Finalize Agreement to Improve Air Quality and Reduce Oil Refinery Flaring in SW Detroit**. An oil refinery operator agreed to improve Southwest Detroit's air quality by spending $6 million to cease operating a flare and another $36 million to mitigate other flare impacts.
2015-16	Department of Health and Human Services	**Partnering to Increase Health Insurance Coverage:** Partnered with the Mayor and Detroit Department of Health and Wellness Promotion to forge a broad and growing coalition focused on increasing health insurance enrollment. During the third open enrollment period, 180,000 Detroiters enrolled in Marketplace health insurance coverage.
2016	Department of Health and Human Services	**Support Substance Use and HIV Prevention Services:** HHS awarded a grant of $1.15 million over five years to help the Teen Hype Youth Development Program provide accessible state-of-the-science substance use and HIV prevention services.
2013-2015	Department of Homeland Security— Federal Emergency Management Agency	**Enabling the Hiring of 150 Firefighters:** In Fiscal Years 2013-2015, the Detroit Fire Department received over $27.3 million dollars from the Assistance to Firefighters Grant Program Branch, which enabled the Detroit Fire Department to hire 150 new firefighters under the Staffing for Adequate Fire and Emergency Response (SAFER) grant program.
2013-2015	Department of Homeland Security— Federal Emergency Management Agency	**Providing for Purchase of Arson Detection and Prevention Equipment and Training:** Detroit received over $1 million to purchase 200 self-contained breathing apparatus (SCBA) and $999,791 for the purchase of a fire training simulator through the Assistance to Firefighters Grant program. Detroit Fire Department also received $731K for the Fire Prevention and Safety grant program that paid for the installation of over 5,000 smoke detectors and the tools and training to aid the department in their goal of investigating every fire.
2015-2016	Department of Housing and Urban Development	**Zero Percent Home Rehab Loans:** HUD and the City of Detroit worked together to develop the "Detroit 0% Interest Home Loan Program." The program provides interest-free loans to Detroit homeowners for home repairs. Loan amounts are between $5K and $25K. HUD provided waivers enabling the City to allocate $6.6 million in HUD CDBG funds and private funders provided $4 million to the program. HUD staff worked closely with the City and LISC, its sub-recipient, on program structure, target areas and other issues.

YEAR	AGENCY/ EXECUTIVE OFFICE	DESCRIPTION
2014-2016	Department of Housing and Urban Development	**Motor City Match—Connecting New & Expanding Businesses with Detroit Real Estate Opportunities:** Motor City Match is a City of Detroit program that uses HUD CDBG funding to connect new and expanding businesses with real estate opportunities by providing rehabilitation assistance to property owners and small business assistance to entrepreneurs. HUD advised on program design to ensure it met local and federal objectives. To date, the program has awarded over $2.9 million in grants to 40 small businesses. In addition, 199 small business owners received help with business plans, 119 with site selections, and 27 with design grants. Of the businesses benefitting from the program: 72 percent are minority-owned businesses, 68% are women-owned businesses, 52 percent are minority owned businesses and 64 percent are Detroit residents.
2014-2016	Department of Housing and Urban Development	**Partnering to Demolish Blight:** A public and private sector effort generated $25.4 million for commercial building demolition. The investments include: • $5 million in Neighborhood Stabilization Program (NSP-3) funding from HUD and the City; • $5.4 million of repurposed CDBG funding from HUD and the City; • $5 million in program income from NSP-2 from the State of Michigan; • $10 million through the fundraising efforts of philanthropic and business organizations.
2014-2016	Department of Housing and Urban Development	**Financing Apartment Development:** Since 2014, the Federal Housing Administration (FHA) has provided mortgage insurance for 14 multi-family development projects, including substantial rehabilitation/new construction for a total of 1,500+ units of affordable and market-rate housing.
2015-2016	Department of Housing and Urban Development	**Expanding Broadband Access**: HUD, through its *ConnectHome* initiative, is partnering with local stakeholders, Comcast, and AT&T to provide 25,000 homes in Detroit with more affordable internet service. Under this program, public housing and HUD-assisted housing residents living in Detroit's Comcast service area will be eligible to apply for "Internet Essentials," the company's high-speed internet adoption program for low-income families.
2014-2016	Department of Housing and Urban Development	**Funds to the Public Housing Authority:** HUD took receivership of the Detroit Housing Commission in 2005. From 2014 to 2016, HUD funded over $16 million in public housing capital funds. The Detroit Housing Commission returned to local control in March 2015.

YEAR	AGENCY/ EXECUTIVE OFFICE	DESCRIPTION
2015-2016	Department of Housing and Urban Development	**Increasing Landlord Participation in HUD's Housing Choice Voucher Program:** Since October 2015, there have been four Landlord Coalition events in Detroit. HUD's Detroit Field Office aimed to recruit new landlords to participate in HUD's Housing Choice Voucher Programs with an emphasis on housing for homeless veterans. Each event includes roundtable discussions, presentations, resource fairs and networking. Detroit is on target to announce an end to veterans' homelessness in April 2017, due in part to this initiative.
2015-2016	Department of Housing and Urban Development	**Appraiser and Underwriter Training Events Geared toward Increasing Mortgage Access:** To spur greater access to credit in Detroit and increase single family mortgage lending, HUD conducted training sessions in 2015 and 2016. Detroiters face trouble qualifying and getting necessary appraisals for residential mortgages, resulting in extremely high rates of sales in cash or by land contract. HUD's FHA staff provided training to single family appraisers and underwriters on minimum property standards, mortgagee responsibility for appraisal integrity, material appraisal deficiencies and single family policy changes. Over 200 local appraisers and underwriters participated in these trainings.
2015-2016	Department of Housing and Urban Development	**Addressing Homelessness: 25 Cities Effort/Mayors Challenge.** In 2015, the City allocated over $5 million in HUD CDBG and ESG funding for housing the homeless. In 2015 and 2016, the City was further allocated $5.5 million in CDBG and HOPWA funds to provide public services to homeless families.
2014-2016	Department of Housing and Urban Development	**Blight Eradication, Land Use and Neighborhood Revitalization:** The City was awarded $18.48 million in HOME funds for affordable housing and $3.4 million in CDBG for emergency repairs to low and moderate income homeowners.
2015	Department of Housing and Urban Development	**Investments in Flood-Preventing Green Infrastructure for the Neighborhoods:** After the August 2014 floods, HUD allocated $8.9 million from the CDBG Declared Disaster Recovery Fund (through a competitive process) to Detroit to be used for green infrastructure to help Detroit neighborhoods better prepare for floods and other natural disasters. The grant targets three Detroit neighborhoods and will be used for: (1) solar energy to back-up the current systems that power the pumps, which expel excess water from flood -prone areas; (2) restoration of a local waterway that will promote new residential and commercial development; and (3) transformation of vacant land into urban landscapes complete with hundreds of bio-swales that will

YEAR	AGENCY/ EXECUTIVE OFFICE	DESCRIPTION
		help manage excess storm water. Physical activities are scheduled to begin in the summer of 2017.
2013-2014	Department of Housing and Urban Development	**Demolished Brewster-Douglass Housing Project, a Symbol of Detroit's Blight Problem:** Used emergency funds to demolish the Brewster-Douglass housing project. The structure had been vacant since 2008. The demolition provided an opportunity for development near downtown.
2016	Department of the Interior- National Park Service (and National Park Foundation)	**Helped Attract Philanthropic Support for Sustainable Recreation at Historic Fort Wayne:** The National Park Service conducted a needs assessment for Detroit's Historic Fort Wayne that identified opportunities for increased recreational use at the military surplus site. The federally-chartered National Park Foundation used this assessment to attract a $350K grant from The Kresge Foundation. For two years, the grant will provide Historic Fort Wayne with a specialist to develop recreation opportunities that complement the site's historic assets.
2015-17	Department of the Interior- National Park Service	**National Park Service Deploys Urban Fellow to Detroit to Provide Technical Assistance Valued at $285K over Two Years:** Technical assistance includes highlighting grant opportunities for Cultural Resource program and facilitating public lands access programs. Active programs include the Land Water Conservation Fund, the Historic Tax Credit, and the River Trails Conservation Assistance Programs.
2015	Department of the Interior- National Park Service	**National Park Service Provides $325K grant from Land Water Conservation Fund to Support Belle Isle Landscape Restoration Efforts:** Funds supported more than 50 acres of revitalization at the athletic field complex.
2015	Department of the Interior- National Park Service	**Building Staff Capacity for Local Conservation Planning:** The National Park Services provided the City $45K to hire a Conservation Legacy Fellow for eleven months. The fellow, who was retained by the city after the end of her fellowship, helped the City create its masterplan for park improvements, among other accomplishments.
2016	Department of Justice	**DOJ Supplements Support for CEASEFIRE Youth Violence Prevention Program:** DOJ awarded $2.1 million in Community-Based Violence Prevention funds to the City of Detroit. The Detroit Police Department plans to continue implementation of CEASEFIRE Detroit, a community outreach and mobilization project launched in 2013 to reduce or eliminate youth-driven gun violence in Detroit neighborhoods and change community norms about the acceptability of violence.

YEAR	AGENCY/ EXECUTIVE OFFICE	DESCRIPTION
2016	Department of Justice	**Addressing Gang Violence with Grant for the Project Safe Neighborhood (PSN) Program:** DOJ awarded $500K to Black Family Development, Inc. for the PSN Task Force, which aims is to reduce gang crime and violence through coordinated suppression, prosecution, community policing, prevention, intervention and treatment. Michigan State University will serve as a research partner: assisting the Task Force in systemic problem solving, data driven interventions, and evaluating the impact of the interventions.
2016	Department of Justice	**Supporting Latina Crime Victim Research Partnership:** A $348K grant will fund a partnership, between Detroit non-profit Community Health and Social Services Center and the Wayne State University School of Social Work to research the culturally-specific mechanisms and services of a Latina victim services program (LA VIDA) in Detroit.
2015 -2016	Department of Justice	**DOJ Provides $3.6 Million Grant Enabling Detroit to Hire 30 Police Offices:** The grant from the DOJ's Community Oriented Policing Services (COPS) Office enables DPD to hire officers who will interact with community organizations and residents to prevent violence. These funds build on previous COPS grants that supported the retention of Detroit police who were in jeopardy of being laid off.
2015	Department of Justice	**Detroit Police Awarded $1 Million to Implement Body-Worn Camera Program:** A Body-Worn Camera program is one tool in the Detroit Police Department's comprehensive problem-solving approach to officer interactions with the public and build community trust. The federal share will cover the cost of 750 BWCs, which is half of the total (1500) that the City will be purchasing to outfit all officers who are deployed to field operations.
2014-2016	Department of Justice	**Detroit Joins Violence Reduction Network as Inaugural Member:** Through the VRN, DOJ provided Detroit expedited access to resources and subject-matter experts to review strengths, promising developments, and identify gaps, unmet needs, and areas for improvement. The specific areas in which Detroit and the DPD indicated critical resource needs to address violence were: (1) youth, gang and drug-related violence; (2) technology support / assessments; (3) homicide reduction; and (4) effective grant strategies.
2013-2016	Department of Justice	**Technical Assistance to Address Consent Decree Requirements, Violence Reduction, Improve Crime Analysis, and Improve Community Policing:** DOJ provided technical assistance to Detroit Police Department with its efforts to improve policing and detention practices meet the requirements of a civil rights consent decree. The consent decrees were terminated in 2014. DOJ helped the city develop

YEAR	AGENCY/ EXECUTIVE OFFICE	DESCRIPTION
		a Crime Analyst training program with Michigan State University to build the city's capacity for data-driven crime analysis. DOJ also provided best practices for reducing youth violence and improving relations between law enforcement and the communities they serve.
2015	Department of Justice	**Detroit Police Awarded $415K for New System to Link Law Enforcement Agencies:** DPD was awarded $415K to implement its Technology Innovation for Public Safety program, a strategic information-sharing system across crime-fighting agencies to address specific local crime problems.
2015	Department of Justice	**Awarding Detroit $720K to Combat Domestic Violence:** The City of Detroit, in partnership with the Detroit Police Department's Domestic Violence Unit, Wayne County Prosecutor's Office, the YWCA Interim House, and LA VIDA will use this award to collaborate in enforcing domestic violence laws; provide services to victims of domestic violence; and improve communication systems.
2015	Department of Justice	**Support for Detroit Community Health Non-Profit Serving Victims of Family Violence and Sexual Assault:** The Community Health and Social Services Center received two awards for $988K to deliver a wide-range of family violence and sexual assault services to adult and youth victims in Southwest Detroit, with a focus on the Latino population.
2014	Department of Justice	**Additional Funding for Detroit's Participation in National Forum on Youth Violence Prevention:** Funding to the City of Detroit increased to a total of $517K. These funds support core youth violence prevention activities.
2014	Department of Justice	**Awarded $355K to Enhance School Safety:** Detroit Public Schools hired three School Resource Officers.
2014	Department of Justice	**DOJ awarded $1 Million to the Big Brothers Big Sisters of Metropolitan Detroit:** Awarded supported Youth Development Prevention and Safety mentoring program.
2016	Department of Labor	**Detroit Awarded $2 Million to Help Provide Summer Jobs for Employment:** Detroit received a $2 million demonstration grant to support workforce training and capacity of the public workforce system, increasing the number of job opportunities through the Mayor's Grow Detroit's Young Talent Initiative (GDYT). These funds support wages and supportive services provided for youth working in summer jobs in summer 2016 and 2017, with the goal of creating career pathways that last beyond summer work.

YEAR	AGENCY/ EXECUTIVE OFFICE	DESCRIPTION
2015-2016	Department of Labor	**Providing Technical Assistance to Support Creation of Mayor's Workforce Development Board:** The Department of Labor provided technical support to newly created Mayor's Workforce Development Board in the form of training on Workforce Innovation and Opportunity Act (WIOA). DOL also provided: (1) technical assistance funding to develop a youth services model that will streamline services delivered to students; and (2) technical assistance to begin the development of a WIOA Adult Integration Services model to serving adults within the public workforce system.
2015	Department of Labor	**Demonstration Grant to Support Workforce Training for Youth, the Long-term Unemployed, and the Formerly-Incarcerated:** Detroit received a $5 million demonstration grant to support workforce training for youth and the long-term unemployed. A portion of the funds are allocated to support an American Job Center within two Detroit correctional facilities and to launch a job preparation program for returning citizens. These efforts are supported locally by Detroit's local, independent My Brother's Keeper initiative.
2011-2017	National Endowment for the Arts	**National Endowment for the Arts -- Providing technical assistance and nearly $300K in creative placement making grants using art and design to transform public spaces in Detroit's Neighborhoods.** Technical assistance led to a grant to nonprofit Greening of Detroit to support landscape design, workforce development and neighborhood revitalization (2016-2017); Landscape arts master plan grant for Sugar Hill neighborhood (2011-2012); Festivals, performances, creative businesses, and storytelling on Hamtramck/Detroit border. (2014-2016); Master plan and designs for multipurpose bike stations for West End's underutilized public parks. (2016-2017); Neighborhood planning and presentation on design and development plans for Bengali immigrant community (2015-2016).
2016-Present	Small Business Administration	**Launching New Pilot Initiative to Provide Entrepreneurial Education and Microloan Access to Formerly-Incarcerated Detroiters:** The *Aspire Entrepreneurship Pilot* is a three-year, $2.1 million public-private partnership between SBA, W.K. Kellogg Foundation, and Justine Petersen, that will provide cohort-based entrepreneurship development and microloan support for citizens returning from incarceration. SBA selected Detroit as one of four pilot locations.

YEAR	AGENCY/ EXECUTIVE OFFICE	DESCRIPTION
2015	Small Business Administration	**Funding Proof of Concept Lab to Support Energy and Transportation Innovation:** NextEnergy earned a $50K prize through the SBA's Growth Accelerator Challenge. The award will help Detroit entrepreneurs commercialize advanced energy and transportation innovations by funding development of Next Energy's Proof of Concept Living Lab.
2013	Small Business Administration	**Organized *American Supplier Initiative* Matchmaker Event to Connect Detroit Small Businesses to New Supply Chains.** ASI is a government-wide federal initiative designed to increase commercial and government supply chain opportunities for small firms. Over 375 small businesses and stakeholders and 42 federal and commercial buyers participated in the half-day event. At least 238 small businesses secured follow-up appointments with buyers.
2015-2016	State Department	**Crafting Detroit's First-Ever Global Engagement Strategy and the Resources for Its Implementation:** The State Department supported the Mayor in developing the City's first-ever Global Engagement Strategy. The strategy includes a plan for a long-term structure for international affairs and areas of potential engagement with federal partners and private partners.
2016	State Department	**Showcasing Detroit Opportunities at Global Entrepreneurship Summit:** The State Department facilitated the "Detroit Story" official partner event at the President's Global Entrepreneurship Summit in Silicon Valley, highlighting Detroit's emerging startup scene before an international audience of entrepreneurs, investors, technologists and policymakers. This was the only city-focused event at GES.
2016	State Department	**Deploying Public and Cultural Diplomacy to Rebuild Detroit's Image Globally:** Worked with the State Department's Bureau of Education and Cultural Affairs to provide technical assistance to local leaders to submit an effective application to the UNESCO Creative Cities program, resulting in Detroit's nomination as the only American city to be designated a UNESCO "City of Design." Worked with US Embassy Rome/Consulate Milan to program engagements with Detroit city leaders at the Venice Architecture Biennale, including with Biennale leadership, the City of Venice, public discussions at the top Architecture School in Venice, and inside the State Department-run American Pavilion—focused historically on four sites currently under development in Detroit. Partnered with the State Department Public Affairs and embassies to organize public outreach and media engagements with local and foreign press in Detroit and overseas during trade missions (e.g. Japan, China, Italy, the Middle East).

YEAR	AGENCY/ EXECUTIVE OFFICE	DESCRIPTION
2015-Present	State Department	**Building Capacity for Trade Missions:** Staffed the Detroit Mayor's first international mission to Japan working with the US Embassy in Japan and numerous federal agencies. Supported the Mayor's second international mission to China, led by the Governor of Michigan. Provided technical assistance for additional city-level engagements in Cuba and Europe working with US Embassies and consulates. Working with federal agencies to provide an export strategy and "best practices" play book for trade missions working with federal partners
2015-Present	State Department with the Department of Housing and Urban Development; the Department of Health and Human Services; and the Department of Homeland Security	**Detroit's First Refugee Resettlement Strategy with Housing Innovation:** Initiated a City-led process to formulate Detroit's first comprehensive refugee resettlement strategy to support resettlement of refugees from Syria and other countries in support the of Administration's policy. Worked with senior leadership in the State Department's Bureau of Population, Refugee, Migration (PRM), the National Security Council (NSC), the White House Domestic Policy Council, DHS, HHS, and HUD. Partnering with HUD on housing options for refugees in Detroit represented a "Detroit" innovation in the refugee resettlement process. Starting in 2016, over 40 families had been resettled in Detroit.
2015	Department of Transportation	**Supporting New Regional Transit Authority with Funding for Rapid Transit:** The DOT provided $6.4 million to RTA to implement a Bus Rapid Transit system that connects Detroit to the metropolitan region.
2014-2015	Department of Transportation	**Providing Detroit Funds and Technical Assistance To Purchase 80 New Buses and Improve Reliability:** A $25 million DOT grant enabled Detroit to purchase 80 new buses and meet the needs of its fixed route service for the first time in decades. There are now 192 buses on the road daily, the most in 20+ years. Twenty-four hour service was recently announced for some key routes. Ridership is up by 25,000 to 50,000 trips weekly since last year.
2010-2014	Department of Transportation	**Innovative Grants Support a Regional Transit Authority and M-1 Rail:** The DOT provided more than $37 million in grants for the new M-1 Rail connecting the Downtown and Mid-Town corridors. The M-1 Rail funding helped motivate the creation of the Regional Transportation Authority (RTA).

YEAR	AGENCY/ EXECUTIVE OFFICE	DESCRIPTION
2013	Department of Transportation	**Unlocking Previously-Awarded DOT Funds:** Ensuring access to $100M in transit grants from DOT, including immediately releasing $24M to repair and rehabilitate buses and install security cameras.
2012	Department of Transportation	**Support for Bike Paths and Other Non-Motorized Transportation:** A $10 million DOT grant was provided for a series of multi-modal infrastructure improvements to create a non-motorized system through the Midtown area to Eastern Market, continuing on to the Detroit River Walk, then extending into downtown Detroit.
2012	Department of Transportation	**"Text My Bus" Initiative:** The federal team collaborated with the city and non-profit organizations, including Code for America and the Knight Foundation, to launch a new mobile initiative that provides better transportation schedules to Detroiters with cell phones, in support of the Mayor's Safe Routes to School and Youth Violence Prevention efforts.
2013-2016	Department of the Treasury	**Stabilizing Neighborhoods and Preventing Avoidable Foreclosures:** As of September 2016, over $64 million of Treasury Department HHF program funds have been disbursed (via the state of Michigan) to assist 6,970 Detroit homeowners. In addition, over $259 million in HHF funds have been allocated fund blight elimination activity in Detroit. The City of Detroit has taken down over 10,000 blighted structures in under two years, over 6,000 of which have been funded by HHF.
2015-2016	Department of the Treasury	**Promoting CDFI Activity in Detroit:** The Community Development Financial Institutions (CDFI) Fund presented an overview of the CDFI Program, the New Markets Tax Credits and Bank Enterprise Award Program, the Capacity Building Initiative, and the Capital Magnet Fund, explaining how these programs could support the strategic growth of CDFIs in Detroit.
2014	Department of the Treasury	**Tax Credits to Finance Streetcar System:** The project's financing has been supported by over $41 million in New Markets Tax Credit allocations by the Department of Treasury's Community Development Financial Institutions Fund.
2013	Department of the Treasury	**Convened a Second Interagency Meeting on Residential Property Vacancy, Abandonment and Demolition.** The Blight Removal Task Force in Detroit presented updates on the work they had done to date, which included the parcel survey they conducted.

YEAR	AGENCY/ EXECUTIVE OFFICE	DESCRIPTION
2016	White House: Community Solutions Team, Office of Social Innovation and Civic Participation; and the Detroit Federal Working Group	**Sharing Data and Best Practices to Improve Public Safety**: In February, the Detroit Police Department joined the White House-led *Police Data Initiative*, a nationwide community of law enforcement agencies committed to opening at least three data sets about policing as a means to increase transparency and accountability and improve community relations. This builds on the open data initiative Mayor Duggan launched in 2015. In October, Detroit joined the White House-led *Data Driven Justice Initiative* coalition of city, county, and state governments that have committed to using data-driven strategies to divert low-level offenders with mental illness out of the criminal justice system and change approaches to pre-trial incarceration, so that low-risk offenders do not remain imprisoned because they cannot afford bail.
2016	White House Detroit Federal Working Group	**Led Working Groups Strategizing to Increase the Demand and Availability of Single-Family Housing:** Detroit's housing stock is overwhelmingly single-family, but would-be Detroit homebuyers face considerable obstacles in their efforts to find and finance move-in ready single family housing. These working groups have generated concept papers with practical strategies to increase the supply of move-in ready homes and to generate demand for home purchases.
2015	White House Detroit Federal Working Group (with the Internal Revenue Service and the General Services Administration)	**Teamed with GSA, IRS and the Mayor to Keep IRS Printing Office in Detroit:** The Mayor visited IRS and GSA when he learned that the IRS was planning to relocate its printing operations to another city. The Congressional delegation, led by Senator Peters, together with local support, made the case to keep the printing office and its 90 jobs in Detroit.
2015	White House Detroit Federal Working Group	**Convening Local Banks, Foundations, Counseling Agencies and the State to Create the *Detroit Home Mortgage*:** The DFWG convened a coalition of banks, foundations, a national CDFI and local counseling agencies to develop a mortgage product that enables Detroiters to purchase a renovated home or a home that requires renovations. The $40 million pool allows applicants to borrow up to $75,000 above appraised value at a 5 percent fixed rate with social investment support from The Kresge Foundation. Homebuyer education is mandatory.

YEAR	AGENCY/ EXECUTIVE OFFICE	DESCRIPTION
2013	White House Office of Science and Technology Policy	**Deploying All-Star Team of Civic Technologists to Help Detroit Find Innovative Tech Solutions:** The White House Office of Science and Technology Policy convened a Tech Team of leading City Chief Technology Officers in Detroit to tackle the biggest technical issues facing the City government. One of these leading technologists, Beth Niblock of Louisville, joined Mayor Duggan's administration as Detroit's Chief Information Officer.

Government-Supported Enterprises

In addition to the contributions of federal agencies, the following contribution was made by government-supported enterprises under the conservatorship of the Federal Housing Finance Agency:

YEAR	CONTRIBUTOR	DESCRIPTION
2014-2016	Government Sponsored Enterprises: Fannie Mae and Freddie Mac (under conservatorship of Federal Housing Finance Agency)	**Fannie Mae and Freddie Mac Launched the *Neighborhood Stabilization Initiative* (NSI) as a Pilot to Assist Detroiters Facing Foreclosure:** Detroit was the first community in which NSI was tested in applying these innovative pre-foreclosure and post-foreclosure strategies as a means of stabilizing selected distressed communities by utilizing the National Community Stabilization Trust. Through NSI, Fannie Mae and Freddie Mac have completed the sale of 481 properties to community-based buyers in Detroit; 131 of these properties were transferred to the Detroit Land Bank for $1 along with demolition contributions of $390K. In addition, Fannie Mae and Freddie Mac have supported struggling Detroit borrowers by providing 238 permanent loan modifications with a low fixed interest rate which reduced payments over 50 percent allowing homes to be saved and neighborhoods to be stabilized.

Acknowledgements

The progress described in this report was made possible by the people of Detroit, its City leaders, and its philanthropies, businesses and community organizations.

The Detroit federal team is grateful to the current and former members of the President's Cabinet whose strong support advanced this new approach to local-federal collaboration: OMB Director Shaun Donovan; Attorney General Eric Holder; Attorney General Loretta Lynch; Secretary Jack Lew; Secretary Timothy Geithner; Secretary Anthony Foxx; Secretary Ray LaHood; Secretary Ernest Moniz; Secretary Steven Chu; Secretary Penny Pritzker; Secretary Thomas Perez; Secretary Hilda Solis; Secretary Julian Castro; Secretary Tom Vilsack; Secretary Sally Jewell; Secretary John Kerry; Secretary Ashton Carter; Secretary Bob McDonald; Secretary Eric Shinseki; Secretary Jeh Johnson; Secretary Janet Napolitano; Secretary Sylvia Mathews Burwell; Secretary Kathleen Sebelius; Administrator Gina McCarthy; Administrator Lisa Jackson; and Administrator Maria Contreras-Sweet.

We especially want to acknowledge the Administration officials who championed the federal efforts in Detroit including: Gene Sperling; Jeffrey Zients; and Cecilia Muñoz. The Detroit Federal Working Group was led by Don Graves, Jr., and Cliff Kellogg. Other Administration officials who supported the work included Derek Douglas, Tara McGuinness, Byron Auguste, Administrator Denise Turner Roth and Chairman Jane Chu. The SC2 Team was led in Detroit by Portia Roberson and nationally by Mark Linton and Patrick Pontius.

Over the years, the federal Detroit teams included: Kerry Duggan; Julie Egan; Jon Grosshans; Danielle Waddell; Nathan Ohle; Tushar Sheth; Kevin O'Connor; Peter Chipman; Elizabeth Garlow; Gina Metrakas; David Dworkin; Sameera Fazili; Jacob Leibenluft; Brandon Belford; Dekonti Mends-Cole; Elizabeth Palazzola; Chris Dorle; Erika Sellke; Dan Lurie; and Denice Ross.

We would also like to thank the members of the Detroit Federal Working Group, including current representatives: Lauren Antelo; Thomas Berry; Raymond Boeman; Katherine Axelsen Braga; Jason Broehm; Brad Carroll; Adam Chepenik; Pete Chipman; Rob Cox; Matt Dalbey; Russella Davis; Norah Deluhery; Beverley Ebersold; Eduard Ekel; Jay Fox; Catherine Gase; David Goldstein; Lauren Dugas Glover; Janet Golrick; Tammie Gregg; Brian Hanes; Beth Hendrix; Adam Honeysett; Allison Johnson; Brian Kamoie; Steve Keck; John Kelly; Michael Kerin; Katie Koehler; John Laswick; Ashley Lewis; Constance Logan; Dan Lurie; Mike Polsinelli; Sika Pryor; Sujeet Rao; Kathryn Reynolds; Mark Rupp; Jason Schupbach; Matthew Stevens; David Thomson; Rosanna Torres; Michelle Werner; Vinn White; Eileen Zaenger; and Nancy-Ellen Zusman.

The Detroit local-federal partnership took a "whole government" approach over its five years; accordingly, thanks are due to many others throughout the federal government.